Columbia University

Contributions to Education

Teachers College Series

No. 388

AMS PRESS
NEW YORK

THE LEGAL CONTROL OF THE ADMINISTRATION OF PUBLIC SCHOOL EXPENDITURES

By

RALPH YAKEL, LL.B., Ph.D.

Teachers College, Columbia University
Contributions to Education, No. 388

Bureau of Publications
Teachers College, Columbia University
NEW YORK CITY
1929

Library of Congress Cataloging in Publication Data

Yakel, Ralph, 1889-
The legal control of the administration of public school expenditures.

Reprint of the 1929 ed., issued in series: Teachers College, Columbia University. Contributions to education, no. 388.
Originally presented as the author's thesis, Columbia.
Bibliography: p.
1. Education--United States--Finance. 2. School management and organization--Law and legislation--United States. I. Title. II. Series: Columbia University. Teachers College. Contributions to education, no. 388.

KF4137.Z9Y3 1972 344'.73'076 78-177618
ISBN 0-404-55388-5

Reprinted by Special Arrangement with Teachers College Press, New York, New York

From the edition of 1929, New York
First AMS edition published in 1972
Manufactured in the United States

AMS PRESS, INC.
NEW YORK, N. Y. 10003

ACKNOWLEDGMENTS

The author wishes to express his appreciation to Dr. N. L. Engelhardt under whose direct guidance and encouragement this study was undertaken and completed. He is indebted also to Dr. Carter Alexander and Dr. J. R. McGaughy for many suggestions as to both the form and the substance of the study. Gratitude is also due Professor Thomas I. Parkinson of the Columbia University Law School for the privilege of visiting certain of his classes in Legislation, which were fertile sources of suggestions with reference to code development.

Many individuals not mentioned personally have greatly aided and facilitated the progress of this study. As this research was principally a documentary study, the aid of the librarians and their assistants in several of the departments of the University was greatly appreciated. Without their prompt assistance in making quickly available the sources of information, this research would have been much more difficult of accomplishment. Especial thanks are due the librarians of the Law School and Teachers College.

A large number of graduate students in the Department of Educational Administration of Teachers College gave the writer their reactions to various phases of the study. These frank statements and criticisms proved a real "testing ground" for evaluating the soundness of the viewpoints and conclusions reached.

CONTENTS

THE LEGAL CONTROL OF THE ADMINISTRATION OF PUBLIC SCHOOL EXPENDITURES

CHAPTER I

INTRODUCTION

The Problem

It is the purpose of this study to offer defensible solutions for the essential elements of the following problem:

What are the most desirable and most effective legal controls which should be established for the regulation of the administration of public school expenditures?

This problem, for the purpose of the investigation, was separated into four minor problems, namely:

1. To determine what legal control is at present exercised over the administration of public school expenditures.
2. To isolate and reveal some of the most important legal principles which have been evolved by the courts and the legislatures for the control of expenditures.
3. To evaluate the present legal control, in the light of research findings and such investigations as are available, and the published opinions of recognized authorities in the fields of education, economics, and political science.
4. To develop and suggest a legal code for the use of those who might seek to enact these findings into law.

Definition of Terms

The term "legal control" as employed in this study is an expression used to designate any restraining or directing influence imposed by the law. When applied to the administration of public school expenditures, it will be considered as any such legal regulation which affects in any degree the educational policies and purposes, or the form and manner of action of any local board of education in the use, management, or accounting for public funds appropriated for educational purposes.

Need for This Study

One special need for this study is the fact that there is a definite trend toward greater state aid to local school districts. Students of educational administration need to be profoundly interested in the nature of the control which will follow such aid. Strayer and Haig[1] point this out in the report of the Educational Finance Inquiry.

> The principle of equality of educational opportunity followed to its logical conclusion is found to arrive at the equivalent of a state educational system, which requires a satisfactory state-wide minimum offering supported by taxes of uniform weight in relation to tax-paying ability throughout the state. This is clearly the destination toward which present forces are tending. The seriousness of the problems to be solved before that destination can be reached should be borne in mind, . . .

The experience of England with its policy of "Grants in Aid" during the past century should be a warning to our people of the natural course which such policies have taken in England, so far as control is concerned.[2] Miss Newcomer,[3] in a recent article, pointed out the fact that in the United States certain policies of aid to different enterprises, such as roads, hospitals, and charitable institutions, have been abandoned because the state no longer controlled such affairs; it had taken them over bodily.

Another need for this type of study is pointed out by one of our foremost legal authorities, Dean Pound[4] of the Harvard Law School, who recently said:

> We are in a period of transition and our legal and judicial institutions are under fire . . . and justly so. And the reason is the same. We are in a period of transition and our legal and judicial institutions, well adapted to and functioning adequately in the society for which they were devised and in which we grew up, are ill adapted to or function at best indifferently, in the society in which they find themselves. . . . We have met this enormous increase of judicial business by multiplying officials, not by reorganizing the administrative side of our tribunals and inventing new methods suitable to the work which they have to do today. . . .
>
> Here the main difficulty is that it is no one's business to study the law functionally, to perceive how and where it falls short, and why; to discover leaks in our apparatus of percepts and doctrines and find out how to stop them. Fifty years ago the judiciary committees of the houses of the legislature were equal to the small amount of investigation of this sort that was required for the efficient functioning of the law. Later committees on law reform in the bar asso-

---

[1] Strayer, G. D., and Haig, R. M., "Financing Education in the State of New York," *Educational Finance Inquiry*, Vol. I, p. 176.

[2] Webb, Sidney, *Grants in Aid*. 1920 Edition. For discussion of these results see *post*, pp. 31ff.

[3] Newcomer, Mabel, "Tendencies in State and Local Finance," *Political Science Quarterly*, March 1928, p. 26.

[4] Pound, Roscoe, "The Present Crisis in American Law," *Harpers*, January 1926, p. 154.

ciations have been able to do part of this task. But today the task has become too great for these agencies. They are not continuously at work. They have no means of surveying the whole field. They can give us but a fraction of their time. We must find some agency which is always in operation, which works under conditions of permanence, independence, and assured impartiality, in which therefore the public may repose confidence.

An authority in the field of public finance (Hunter)[5] has stated the need for further studies in the problems of public expenditure:

> Only recently do we find fiscal students turning serious attention to the problems of public expenditure. Comparatively little literature can be found dealing with this phase of public finance, while volumes have been written on methods of securing revenue.
>
> It is impossible, however, to segregate the two fields. If funds are squandered and wasted the best possible revenue system cannot give satisfactory results. . . . A further recent demand is that the administration of public funds be handled in an efficient manner.

Limitation of the Problem

The necessity of limiting a problem in this field of investigation is obvious. There are closely related, easily recognized controls and very subtle remote controls exercised over school expenditures by our legal system. Every problem of fiscal administration might be logically connected with a study of a control of expenditures. It was decided to limit this study to an intensive investigation of certain phases of the problem. The selection has been made rather carefully, yet to a degree somewhat arbitrarily. The fact that a rather extensive survey of all the problems involved was made before the limitations were made has been one check, and to a degree an evaluation of the topics selected. The exact method used in selecting the topics to be discussed is described in step (IV) of the "Method of Attack."[6] The reasons for eliminating certain of the more closely related topics which might have been treated more extensively are stated briefly.

Since Henzlik[7] had made his thorough study of Capital Outlay Contracts and had gone into certain phases of the administration of bond funds, the elimination of a detailed study of expenditures for capital outlay could be eliminated without detracting from the value of this study. However, when building funds are used for current expenses or current expense funds for building purposes,

[5] Hunter, M. H., *Outlines of Public Finance*, p. 22.

[6] See *post*, pp. 5ff.

[7] Henzlik, F. E., *Rights and Liabilities of Public School Boards Under Capital Outlay Contracts.*

the matter becomes one of another type of control and is treated in this study.

It was planned that all reference to income and tax levy control over the sources of funds would be avoided, but, in the development of the code, it was found impossible to separate the control exercised over the purposes and methods of expenditure by control over income from that thereafter exercised over the expenditure budget. It has been necessary, therefore, to use the findings and research of Frasier,[8] McGaughy,[9] Young,[10] and others who have made contributions to this field and reduce the same to code provisions. Repetition of the findings made by these researches is avoided so far as possible and discussion is given in detail only where this or other research has contributed additional information.

Other problems recognized and closely related, but not exhausted in this study, are considered only in their larger aspects. The following problems are of this class and offer to other research workers many opportunities for study:

1. *Borrowing Money.* This research will be interested only in the law concerning the general administration of a borrowing plan as it may relate to a control of the purposes and policies of a school system. There are many other problems in this immediate field, and the courts are much confused upon many phases of these problems. Halsey[11] quotes seventeen typewritten pages of statutory enactment and decisions of the courts in his study made concerning the borrowing of money in the State of Florida.

   Bonds. A casual glance into the field of the issue and administration of bond funds seems to indicate some important legal problems needing intensive study.

2. What constitutes an "educational expenditure," as the courts define it, is worthy of an extensive research into its legal implications. This study will concern itself with the general administration of educational policies and not as to the details of exactly what the courts have decided to be legal or illegal expenditures.

3. The care and custody of funds is another problem closely related, but is not considered an essential phase of the control of expenditures. A study of this problem is being made concurrently with this study.[12]

[8] Frasier, G. W., *The Control of City School Finance.*
[9] McGaughy, J. R., *Fiscal Administration of City School Systems.*
[10] Young, D. S., *Control of Available Public School Income.*
[11] Halsey, H. R., *Borrowing Money for the Public Schools.*
[12] Linn, H. H., *Safeguarding School Funds.*

Method of Attack

I. The first step was to make the usual preliminary study necessary before any serious investigation could be undertaken. The steps in this preliminary study were made in the following order: (1) bibliography preparation; (2) reading and study extensive and thorough enough to be sure of the researches already done in this and closely related fields; (3) limiting the problem; and (4) outlining the study.

II. The second step was the making of a comprehensive study of the decisions of the courts of record of cases originating in problems involving the administration of public school expenditures. There were several steps in this procedure:

1. An orientation in the field of law was made by a study of law books and digests covering this entire field of control of expenditures. Ruling Case Law, Cyc, American Law Reports, Corpus Juris, and treatises upon Municipal Corporations, such as those by Dillon and McQuillin, were examined for the purpose of finding what information had already been drawn together and to find possible cues for the treatment of the topic and study.
2. An index of topics which might have some relation to control was made. This list of topics is given in Appendix B.
3. A search was made under each of the headings mentioned in (2) in the American Digest System for cases bearing upon the topics. The American Digest System claims to list (and it is recognized as approximating this ideal) under general headings and under cross-references all the cases decided in courts of record in the United States. On the first checking, decisions for the past ten years were listed. The latest index available was complete to July 1928.
4. The cases listed were then read and digested. The most recent cases were read first. The leading cases cited in these decisions were read at this time also.
5. Shepard's Citators [13] were used to check up each case as it was read to find out if the decision had been upheld, reversed, modified, or cited in subsequent judicial action. If the decision was cited, such cases were read, citations taken again, and so on until the law of the courts was known.

[13] Shepard's Citators are publications issued quarterly, with monthly supplements, for each division of the American Digest System and are so arranged as to give the exact reference where any court mentions, in any way, the decisions cited. Tracing down citations of this type leads one into all sorts of cases, and after doing this reading one is fairly certain that the principle of the law thus traced is the law.

6. Certain topics which, reading up to this point, indicated to be of fundamental importance were traced back through all the digests of the American Digest System. These cases were read, digested, and traced back to the first statement of the principle involved. Thus was the law of the courts revealed. This was, of course, an extremely laborious process, but the recompense comes in seeing the law develop. Interest was not hard to maintain because the courts have every conceivable type of problem confronting them, even in so prosaic a topic as control of expenditures.

III. The third step was the making and application of a checking list for the study of the statutory law relating to public school expenditures. The results of this work furnished the investigator with certain facts of and trends in legislation which were great aids in gaining an understanding of the case law studied. The statutory regulations were used just as the case studies were, to show the status and trends of the law.

IV. The fourth step was the selection of the decisions to be used. As the value of this study depended to some extent upon the type of cases selected, a description of the bases used in the selection of the decisions cited in this study is set forth in some detail.

The first task was to select the general principles which were to be used as the basic points to be treated. At this point in the procedure the investigator had a large number of decisions (approximately 1,000) from many and divers divisions of the law relating to the control of school expenditures. A choice had to be made as to the most important topics to be reported. These general divisions, together with the minor topics, were chosen principally upon the following two bases:

1. *Importance to school administration.* It would obviously be useless to report cases and decisions which did not represent important issues in the administration of school expenditures. The decisions were classified in accordance with the most important issues involving practice, theory, and principle which have engaged the attention of students of educational administration. Particular attention was paid to decisions of the courts which are opposed to the commonly accepted principles of school administration.
2. *Frequency of issues arising in the courts.* Cases involving a similar set of particulars appearing frequently in the courts is evidence that the law is not reaching the fundamental prin-

ciples involved. Therefore, the number of decisions involving a particular point of law was a criterion used for the inclusion of representative cases from such groups. There were several instances, however, where but a single case was reported which involved principles of great importance. Such "sporadic" cases in a field such as school administration quite often point out principles of the law, which might not otherwise be brought to the attention of students of educational administration until after such principles had secured a standing in the courts.

After the selection of the type or class of decisions to be studied and reported, a choice had to be made of the individual decisions which were to be quoted. In making this choice another set of criteria had to be used. The object in view was to select the strongest decision possible to present a particular point of view, and, when there were serious differences of opinion, to find the decisions which would present this opposed viewpoint most strongly. The bases used were:

1. *Jurisdiction.* Certain jurisdictions have greater weight than others. For example, New York, Illinois, Michigan, and California are representative of states which are regarded as jurisdictions from which the decisions of their courts have great weight as precedents with the courts of other states. Therefore, as between two jurisdictions, the court of the state having the greatest weight was selected. However, when more than one decision involving a particular point of law was to be reported, the decisions were selected from as diverse jurisdictions as possible.

2. *Date of decision.* When the principle of law was the chief thing most desired to be presented, the earliest decision is usually the best. The court which has to decide a point of law for the first time is establishing precedent and is aware of the fact that other judges will pick the decision to pieces, if it is not fortified with strong argument and sound reasoning. Such a court therefore has to make a thorough study of the points involved and cite them so that other courts will know just what evidence lies behind the decision.

   When the law which at present controls was the principal thing desired, the latest decisions available obviously presented the rule most likely to be followed.

3. *Clarity and definiteness of decision.* When decisions are otherwise equal, the decision which is most definite, clearest, and most specific in enunciating the principle of law was chosen.

V. The fifth step was to evaluate the law of the legislatures and of the courts with the results of available research in the fields of education, law, political science, and economics.

VI. The sixth step was to develop the proposed code and reduce the findings to writing.

The research value of this type of a study and the methods of attack are indicated by a statement of Freund:[14]

> That a statute becomes the subject matter of litigation regularly indicates some difficulties encountered in its application, and may suggest methods or principles of legislation, whereby the difficulty might have been avoided.

This study is an endeavor to find out the type and substance of the law and the administrative organization which will be so constituted that the administrative authorities will be stimulated and inspired to the most desirable management of school expenditures. A second task is to find the most effective remedies which will insure, by the use of the strong arm of the law, if necessary, the protection of the public interest.

The law cannot lift itself by means of "pulling at its own bootstraps." Neither may it be expected that results will be produced simply by changing the code of laws. Such a procedure would be analogous to painting a pump a different color, hoping thereby to produce a different quality of water. These procedures are all too common in legislative enactments. In the growth of the law, the influences of science and social conditions have always had a hard task to secure proper recognition. It is true that the law will finally, after many experiments in legislation, arrive at a conclusion which, in most cases, will represent the evolution of the best thoughts of the people. This is the way the common law developed. We cannot wait in this day of rapidly changing conditions for such slow procedure to take place.

As indicated by Dean Pound, we are to face a new development of legal institutions. The need of this type of research is further indicated by other authorities on the subject of legal science.

> It is a truly remarkable situation that with the greatest development of legal learning there is the scantiest knowledge of the operation of legal rules. Lawyers, lawmakers, and law teachers are occupied with the conceptual problems produced in great abundance by the creation of legal rules, but, strangely

[14] Freund, Ernst, *Science of Legal Method*, p. 582.

enough, they do not know how these rules are being realized, if at all, in actual life.[15]

This leaves the way "wide open" to the men and women engaged in the study of education to conduct their own research in this field. It is hoped that there may be some suggestions in this study which will attract more workers into this fertile field of research.

[15] Freund, Ernst, *Science of Legal Method*, p. vii, Preface.

CHAPTER II

LEGAL RELATION BETWEEN THE STATE AND THE SCHOOL DISTRICT

The following principles of the law relating to the legal control which the state may exercise over the local school district are to be discussed in this chapter.

I. School districts are subject to any regulation which the legislature may make concerning their powers, rights, and liabilities, provided the legislature does not overstep the limitations imposed by the Constitution of the United States or the Constitution of the State.

II. The general rule is that the legislature can, subject only to constitutional restrictions, direct that local or state funds for educational purposes shall be expended in accordance with legislative direction.

III. Local school districts are held by the courts of most of the states to be corporate bodies (quasi-corporations) whch are corporations of a lower grade than those known as municipal corporations.

IV. Statutes regulating school affairs are usually interpreted very strictly by the courts.

V. The general rule is that when the legislature confers the power upon a board of education to do any particular act and the exercise of such power requires discretion, the courts will not question the exercise of such discretion except for fraud, collusion, or capricious action.

VI. Constitutional provisions concerning the organizations and powers of the several divisions of the public school system have in numerous instances handicapped the establishment of a desirable and flexible state and local administrative organization of the schools.

Schools Are Subject to the Will of the State

I. School districts are subject to any regulation which the legislature may make concerning their powers, rights, and liabilities, provided the legislature does not overstep the limitations imposed by the Constitution of the United States or the Constitution of the State.

Lest there be any question as to the relation of the school district to the state, some decisions upon the point are given. The decisions are cited as evidence that the state may make any regulation it may desire to make concerning the schools within its boundaries. The only exceptions to the above rule are the limitations imposed by the Constitution of the United States, the Constitution of the State, or a referendum of the people.

A decision by one of America's foremost jurists, Judge Cooley, rendered in 1873, has greatly influenced other courts in making their rulings upon the legal relation of the local to the state government.

> In all matters of general concern there is no local right to act independently of the State. . . . And we concur fully in the views which have been expressed by other courts in the cases to which our attention was called on the argument, that as regards the duties which the people in the several localities owe the Commonwealth at large, they cannot be allowed a discretionary authority to perform them or not as they may choose. Such an authority would be wholly inconsistent with anything like regular or uniform government in the State.[1]

The latest case in point reported is from Colorado (1928).

> A school district is a subdivision of the state for educational purposes. The several officers charged with the supervision from the State Board down to the directors of the school district, are merely instruments of the state government, chosen for the purpose of effectuating its policy in relation to schools. . . . The school district is created as a means for the more convenient and effective carrying out of the educational policy of the state. The entire control of schools and school property is in the state, to be exercised as it may see fit, subject to the requirements and restrictions contained in the Constitution; the school officers and school districts are merely the agencies through which it acts in the performance of duties which it is charged by that instrument.[2]

The leading case in this field and a case which has probably been more often quoted than any other single case is that of State *v.* Howarth,[3] in which the principle that a school is a state institution was strongly enunciated.

Case after case might be cited to further emphasize this point, but the limits of this study (interesting as this phase may be) will not permit an elaborate treatment of this point. This

---

[1] People *v.* Common Council Detroit, 28 Mich. 228, 15 Am. Rep. 202.

[2] Olson Lumber Co. *v.* School District No. 8, 83 Colo. 272, 263 P. 723. Upholding Florman *v.* School Dist., 6 Colo. App. 319, 40 P. 469, 1895.

[3] State *v.* Howarth, 122 Ind. 462, 23 N. E. 946 (1890).

study is more concerned with the practical application of this principle to the control of school expenditures which will be treated in the next section.

The Power of the Legislature Over School Expenditures

II. The general rule is that the legislature can, subject only to constitutional restrictions, direct that local or state funds for educational purposes shall be expended in accordance with legislative direction.

The exercise of the power of control over expenditures, even to the extent of dictating that the school district must make certain expenditures, was stated extremely well in the case of McMillan *v.* Clarke:

> It may well be questioned if the imposition of financial burdens upon the school districts, by the general laws, for the maintenance of public schools comes within the restriction of the Constitution against taxation for local or municipal purposes. The public schools are state schools, and it is within the discretion of the legislature whether to make them a charge upon the state at large, or to do as has been done in the matter of elementary schools, make them a charge partly upon the state at large and partly upon the local districts, or, as in the case of high schools, place practically the entire burden upon a district organized for that purpose.
>
> . . . In other words, in dealing with these local municipal agencies for conducting the state administration, the legislature reserves the right to impose burdens, which must be met by local tax levies.[4]

The Pennsylvania Supreme Court rendered as part of a decision in 1925 the following opinion:

> Aside from constitutional restrictions, the legislature is the sole judge of the wisdom, expedience, and necessity for expending the state's money, the amount to be expended, the inauguration of the policy of government under which it is spent. . . . The judiciary cannot run a race of opinions upon points of right, reason, and expediency with the law-making power.[5]

A succinct summary of the legislature's authority is given by a legal authority.

> The power of appropriation which a legislature can exercise over the revenues of the state for any purpose, which it may regard as calculated to promote the public good, it can exercise over the revenues of a county, city, or town, for any purpose connected with the present or past condition, except as such revenues may by the law creating them be devoted to special purposes.[6]

---

[4] McMillan *v.* Clarke, 184 Cal. 491, 194 P. 1030 (1920). A. L. R. 17: 288.

[5] Busser *v.* Snyder, 282 Pa. 440, 128 A. 80.

[6] Smith, J. W., *Modern Law of Corporations*, Vol. I, sec. 758.

Illustrations of the Legislative Power

The legislature of Louisiana wrestled with a problem of paying teachers who worked in New Orleans during the years 1874, 1875, and 1876. Outstanding claims have been in the courts up to as recently as 1924. In 1912 and also in 1914 special acts were passed by the legislature to provide for the enforcement of the payment of judgments which had been rendered as early as 1892. These acts required that the parish of New Orleans should run the schools on 95 per cent of the revenue collected and that the remaining 5 per cent should be applied toward the payment of claims which had been reduced to judgment. A Federal Court upheld the right of the legislature to pass such an act.[7]

The city of Memphis, Tennessee, was required by the legislature to admit pupils to the city schools, even though they lived outside the city limits. This was a temporary measure and applied only to pupils living within one half-mile of the city, but the reasoning of the court in upholding the legislative right to pass such a law calls attention to possibilities and the extent to which the state control may follow state aid.

> It is well settled that such a corporation is under the control of the legislature, so that it may be abolished, or its power or its responsibilities increased, at any time, by that body, without the danger of encountering constitutional difficulties. . . . Not only is this true, but the board depends largely for the maintenance of its schools upon sources of income found outside the limits of the city of Memphis. Independent of the property and poll taxes levied by the city authorities for this purpose, it receives from the state its proper proportion of the moneys derived from the payment of interest on the common school fund, as well as from the poll and property tax imposed and collected by the state for school purposes, and the poll tax and the tax on property levied and collected by the County of Shelby for the same purpose . . .[8]

Black, in his *Handbook of American Constitutional Law* (p. 500), draws the conclusion that the state legislature, in the absence of constitutional limitations, may exercise extreme powers over the finances of a municipal corporation. This conclusion would apply with equal force to school districts:

> The legislature has power to require a municipal corporation to pay its just debts, even when they are not enforceable by the ordinary processes of law, and to this end may require the municipality to raise money by taxation.

[7] Fisher *v.* Orleans Parish, 229 F. 1 (1916).

[8] Edmonson *v.* Board of Education, Memphis, 108 Tenn. 557, 69 S. W. 274 (1902).

The legislature of Massachusetts required the city of Lowell to appropriate money toward the establishment of a textile school.[9]

A recent case in North Dakota upheld the right of the state to establish a state fire and tornado insurance company which is so organized as to make it compulsory for school districts to take out their insurance in this state company. This is the first case of this kind and in effect makes the school district contract with a state agency for its fire insurance. The principle is important, for, if the state can require school districts to contract with it for one thing, it may do so for many other things.[10]

The Kentucky Court of Appeals, however, would not uphold an act of the legislature which required the city of Covington to appropriate three mills of its thirty-five mill tax levy to the establishment of a public library.

> But it is easy to see that if a percentage of the amount levied and collected for school purposes may be diverted to every object which indirectly aids the "cause of education," "the general system of education," the tax for school purposes might be raised to the legislative limit without obtaining a sufficient amount to pay teachers and maintain the buildings.[11]

The power of the legislature to fix minimum salaries has been upheld[12] and also the power to direct that women teachers be paid salaries equal to the salaries paid to men teachers,[13] provided they are doing the same type of work.

Legal Status of School Districts—General

III. Local school districts are held by the courts of most of the states to be corporate bodies (quasi-corporations) which are corporations of a lower grade than those known as municipal corporations.

School districts have been held by the courts to be municipal corporations in New York,[14] Illinois,[15] Texas,[16] and West Virginia.[17]

[9] Hanson *v.* Lowell, 165 Mass. 419, 43 N. E. 196 (1896).

[10] Minot Special School District *v.* Olsness, 53 N. D. 683, 208 N. W. 968, 45 A. L. R. 1337 (1926).

[11] Board of Education Covington *v.* Board of Trustees Public Library, 113 Ky. 234, 68 S. W. 10 (1902).

[12] Moore *v.* Board of Education City of New York, 106 N. Y. S. 983 (1926).

[13] Moses *v.* Board of Education Syracuse, 217 N. Y. S. 265, 127 Misc. Rep. 477 (1926).

[14] Caldwell *v.* Board of Education, 216 N. Y. S. 501 (1926).

[15] Stroh *v.* Casner, 201 Ill. App. 281 (1916).

[16] Chrestman *v.* Tompkins, Texas, 5 S. W. 2nd, 257 (1928).

[17] Krutuli *v.* Board of Education, 99 W. Va. 466, 129 S. E. 486 (1925).

The statutes so designate them in Indiana, Iowa, and Oregon. It should be noted that even though the statutes designate the districts as municipal corporations in Iowa [18] and Oregon,[19] cases have recently been decided which place them in the quasi-corporation category.

Connecticut [20] subjects the school district to the same laws as those applying to town officials or boards. California seems to classify the school districts as divisions of the state.[21]

A recent Minnesota case held that the board of education of Duluth was a department of the city government.[22]

In the rest of the states, school districts are by statutory enactment or by interpretation of the statutes by the courts designated as a "body corporate."

In Iowa it was said:

> School boards have no powers except such as are conferred by legislative act, either expressly or by necessary implication, and doubtful claims of power are resolved against them.[23]

This decision coming from a state which designates by statute that the school district is a municipal corporation is especially significant as to the rigid requirements which a code regulating the affairs of a school district must meet. This rigid interpretation has been upheld in Washington [24] and in Wisconsin [25] and by the courts of many other states.

Interpretation of Statutes

IV. Statutes regulating school affairs are usually interpretated very strictly by the courts.

The legal status of school districts has been shown rather fully for the purpose of determining certain principles of code development, which will be necessary to an understanding of some of the reasoning underlying the code being here developed. The definition of powers given to municipal corporations is well

---

[18] Courtright *v.* Consolidated Independent District Mapleton, 203 Iowa 26, 212 N. W. 368 (1927).

[19] Jacoberger *v.* School District No. 1, 122 Ore. 124, 256 P. 652 (1927).

[20] Lucier *v.* Town Norfolk, 99 Conn. 639, 122 A. 711 (1923).

[21] Esberg *v.* Badaracco, Cal., 259 P. 730 (1927).

[22] State *ex rel.* Pine *v.* Board of Education Duluth 159 Minn. 62, 197 N. W. 964 (1924).

[23] Andrew *v.* Stuart Savings Bank, 204 Iowa 570, 215 N. W. 807 (1927). Reaffirming Bopp *v.* Clark, 165 Iowa 697, 52 L. R. A., 493.

[24] Hansen *v.* Lee, 119 Wash. 691, 206 P. 927 (1922).

[25] Town of Swiss *v.* U. S. National Bank, Wisconsin, 218 N. W. 842 (1928).

stated by Dillon, one of the leading legal authorities on this subject:

It is a general and undisputed proposition of law that a municipal corporation possesses and can exercise the following powers and no others:

First, those granted in express words.

Second, those necessarily or partly implied in or incident to the powers expressly granted.

Third, those essential to the accomplishment of the declared purposes and objects of the corporations—not simply convenient, but indispensable.[26]

Concerning the powers of school districts which he classifies as quasi-corporations Dillon says:

It is but an instrumentality of the state, and the state incorporates it that it may effectually discharge its appointed duty. . . . They are involuntary political or civil divisions of the state created by general laws to aid in the administration of government. . . . Considered with respect to the limited number of their corporate powers, the bodies above rank low down in the scale or grade of corporate existence; and hence have often been termed quasi-corporations. This designation distinguishes them, on the one hand, from private corporations aggregate, and, on the other hand, from municipal corporations proper.[27]

It must therefore be kept in mind that statutes which are intended to regulate expenditures must be very carefully written, so as to grant the exact powers intended to the governing bodies of school districts. This strict interpretation of the courts upon the powers granted to schools is one reason why legislation in that realm has been so detailed—the law-makers having earnestly sought to confer a great variety of powers upon the school boards. How well they have succeeded is shown by a case originating in Ohio, where the judge seemed to doubt the advisability of giving them too much power, but stated the legal situation in very strong terms.

It will be concluded that under our present school law, Boards of Education are given almost unlimited power. The remedy is not in the courts, but with the legislature. If these laws do not meet the approval of the people, they should appeal to the legislature of Ohio to amend or repeal such as are not in accord with sound public sentiment.[28]

Discretion Granted to Boards of Education

V. The general rule is that where the legislature confers the power upon a board of education to do any particular act and the

[26] Dillon, *Municipal Corporations*, Vol. 1, sec. 237, pp. 448–51, 1911 (5th ed).

[27] *Ibid.*, p. 66.

[28] Stinson *v.* Board of Education, 17 Ohio App. 437 (1923).

exercise of such power requires discretion, the courts will not question the exercise of such discretion except for fraud, collusion, or capricious action.

Once a power has been given to a board of education by the legislature to do any particular thing, the courts have been inclined to give it rather broad powers of discretion, and usually the courts will not interfere unless there is a "clear abuse of discretion."[29]

The abuse of discretion . . . implies not merely an error of judgment but perversity of will, passion, or moral delinquency; and its decisions must be final, except when its action is capricious or arbitrary.[30]

But the exercise of an honest judgment, though erroneous, is not an abuse of discretion.[31]

Discretion of Boards of Education as Applied to Expenditure of Money

It is very difficult for statutes to set out in exact terms the powers of the board to make expenditures and at the same time leave with the board a freedom of action which is generally accepted as being highly desirable. The law reports are full of cases involving the discretionary power of boards of education to make expenditures. What is an expenditure for educational purposes? In this day of rapidly advancing curricula, what today may seem a questionable activity requiring expenditure of funds, tomorrow may be the common practice. As it is, every new activity has to fight its way through the courts, until some judge will take judicial notice of advanced conditions and allow it to be a charge upon the public purse. The exact determination of the rules which govern and distinguish between legal and illegal expenditures of funds is worthy of an extended research. This study will consider simply some of the general principles which the courts have deduced, and which they use as guideposts through this complex field.

The expenditure of the funds within the statutory limits is entirely within the discretion of the board of education. . . . In short, the objects mentioned in the statute for which the board of education may expend funds under its control comprehends all the educational needs of the county. The State intended to, and does, invest the board of education with a large discre-

[29] *Ruling Case Law*, Vol. 24: 575. Also 48 A. L. R. 654 (1926).

[30] Williams *v.* Board of Education Parsons, 79 Kan. 202, 99 P. 216 (1908).

[31] Tug and Wrecking Co. *v.* County Board of Education, 75 Mich. 360, 42 N. W. 968 (1889).

tion in the expenditure of the funds levied for the benefit of the schools, and so long as this discretion is not abused, or is reasonably exercised, the courts will not interfere with it.[32]

Judge Davis of the New York Court of Appeals said:

Under the duties with which it is charged, the board must make the final decision as to how the money within its control shall be expended in providing an efficient system of education, with high regard for the proper instruction, protection of health, and general welfare of the children committed to its charge. In its powers and activities it is limited only by the amount of funds within its control, and by definite provisions of law pertaining to the use of such funds.[33]

A recent New Mexico case states a very liberal opinion and gives an extremely broad interpretation of the powers of the board in determining school policies. The case concerned the power of the board to purchase life insurance, on the group plan, for its teachers. This has been the only case involving this question decided in any of the states.

The expenditure of public funds raised by taxation or other methods for public purposes must necessarily be intrusted by the legislature to public agencies, and these agencies are required to exercise discretion and judgment in determining the purpose for which such money will be spent, within the limits of the authority granted, and the courts will not interfere unless there is a clear departure from the legislative authority. In the management and conduct of public schools of the state the school authorities are called upon to determine the objects and purposes for which school funds shall be expended, within the limits of the authority granted, which will prove beneficial to and promote the interests of education, and to expend money daily for such purposes.[34]

However, this is one of the most liberal decisions rendered and it cannot be hoped that it will be followed in other jurisdictions except as the law slowly evolves. The remedy will be found much more quickly in carefully writing the code covering this point.

The distinction between the court's control of the board in the exercise of its statutory powers and its power to act under such a statute is well expounded in the following case:

The question before us is not whether the defendant board is properly exercising its statutory discretion, but whether it is exceeding its statutory power. The question of discretion is not subject to judicial control. But the question of statutory power is subject to judicial control.[35]

[32] Fiscal Court Logan County *v.* Board of Education Logan County, 138 Ky. 98, 127 S. W. 527 (1910).

[33] Rief *v.* Schwab, 204 N. Y. App. 50 (1922).

[34] Nohl *v.* Board of Education Albuquerque, 27 N. M. 232, 199 P. 373 (1921).

[35] Schmidt *v.* Blair *et al.*, 203 Iowa 1,016, 213 N. W. 593 (1927).

Texas announces:

The legislature has sought to place the public free school system in a position of freedom from interference as far as practicable.[36]

The New York courts are emphatic in giving wide powers under the statutes to boards of education.

In the conduct of the public schools it is essential that power be vested in some legalized agency in order to maintain discipline and promote efficiency. In considering the exercise of this power, the courts are not concerned with the wisdom or unwisdom of the act done. The only concern of the court is the reasonableness of the regulation promulgated. To hold otherwise would be to submit judicial opinion for the legislative will.[37]

In Campbell *v.* New York City the court said:

The courts do not sit in judgment upon the questions of legislative policy or administrative discretion. The taxpayer must point to illegality or to fraud.[38]

The discretion of the county board was upheld in Alabama,[39] but the courts will interfere in Arkansas to prevent funds being used for purposes other than support of the public schools.[40]

An examination of the statutes of the several states discloses the fact that most of the states have been more or less specific in designating the purposes for which public money may be expended. Florida, Idaho, Kansas, Kentucky, Maryland, Michigan, Missouri, Nevada, Utah, Ohio, South Dakota, and Washington each have a clause or section in their statutes which attempts to confer general powers of determining what constitutes an expenditure for education in addition to various specific purposes for which money may be expended. North Carolina, Louisiana, and Wyoming have only a general clause and confer absolute power upon local districts to determine the purposes for which they will expend their funds. Pennsylvania prohibits expenditures for anything not in the act regulating schools.

At the present time under the interpretation of the courts, it is very difficult to avoid the specification of all the items of expenditure for which it will be legal for boards of education to use public funds. The decisions of the courts as to what are

[36] Underwood *v.* Sabinal Independent School District, Texas, 285 S. W. 267 (1925).

[37] Flory *v.* Smith (N. Y.) 134 N. E. 360, A. L. R. 36: 654 (1926).

[38] Campbell *v.* New York City, 244 N. Y. 317, 155 N. E. 628 (1928).

[39] King *v.* County Board of Education Russell County, 214 Ala. 620, 108 So. 588 (1926).

[40] County Board of Education *v.* Austin, 169 Ark. 436, 276 S. W. 2 (1925).

proper expenditures for the furtherance of education in any given state would be a large study in itself.

When general powers to make expenditures are granted, the result is that every item of expenditure may have to run the gamut of the courts. The only other alternative is to set up a new type of legal machinery to regulate expenditures. This might be done by delegating the specification of expenditures to the State Board of Education. This alternative will be discussed more fully under the powers granted to the State Board of Education and to the State Commissioner of Education.[41]

State Constitutional Provisions

VI. Constitutional provisions concerning the organizations and powers of the several divisions of the public school system have in numerous instances handicapped the establishment of a desirable and flexible state and local administrative organization of the schools.

The efforts made by many of the makers of the state constitutions to insure that certain rights be retained by the people have been, in many instances, hindrances and undue handicaps to freedom of the legislative action. In the light of present-day scientific knowledge of educational administration, these restrictions have been serious handicaps to educational progress. The constitution makers placed the provisions in the constitution because they believed the policies to be fundamental. Certain of these policies have had to be abandoned as time progressed and as knowledge has increased. A reference to a few instances will be sufficient to establish this point.

Many states wishing to adopt state aid or equalization laws which would tend to aid in the establishment of a policy of equalization of educational opportunity are today hindered in the adoption of such policies because the constitution provides that state funds must be distributed "uniformly," "in proportion to the population," "according to the census enumeration" or provisions having similar effect. Eighteen of the states have some such provision which handicaps the proper distribution of at least some of the state funds.[42]

---

[41] *Post,* p. 35 ff. Also Proposed Code, Art. IV, sec. 2, subdiv. d.

[42] Ala., Ariz., Tex., Fla., Iowa., Ky, La., Minn., Miss., N. M., N. D., S. D., Ore., Okla., Utah, Va., Wis., and Wyo.

The famous Kalamazoo case [43] had to be fought out in the courts before a legal precedent was established for the expenditure of funds for high schools. This principle had to be tried out in a great many other states before the matter was fully accepted as the law, and the only way that the older states could be absolutely certain that expenditures for high schools were legal was to try the matter out in the courts. Today the junior college is developing and its establishment may be unconstitutional in some of the states where the funds must be used for the "common" schools. All of the states do have a provision that the income from the permanent school funds shall be used for the support of the "common" or "public" schools.[44] This means that the establishment of every new type of school, or every curriculum change of major importance, in some states, may have to go through the courts and be classified as a common or public school function in order that state school funds may be used for this purpose. In some of the states, however, new sources of income may be made available for the new types of schools or curricula, but this is too precarious a foundation on which to build. This is true even though the term "'Common Schools' means schools open to all, rather than those of any particular grade." [45]

Today we are in a period in which preschool and formal adult education are both seemingly desirable, but, under present constitutional provisions definitely fixing the ages of those to be a part of the common schools, provisions for such types of educational institutions will have to await amendments to the state constitution. Fifteen states decree that public schools shall be established for children between certain ages.[46]

In order to avoid the handicaps which have been imposed by too rigid provisions in the state constitutions, the following two sections are proposed as desirable sections of the state constitution if such changes become possible. The sections submitted are sufficient to cover any desirable control of expenditures which may be proposed by the legislature. These sections are not intended to be all-inclusive as covering many other possible

---

[43] Stuart *v.* School District No. 1, Village Kalamazoo, 30 Mich. 69 (1872).

[44] Index to State Constitutions, Legislative Drafting Bureau, Columbia University, p. 554.

[45] Roach *v.* Board of Education, 77 Mo. 484 (1883).

[46] Data taken from Index to State Constitutions, *op. cit.* Ala., Ariz., Ark., Colo., La., Miss., Mo., Mont., Neb., N. J., N. C., Pa., S. C., Wis. and N. M.

rights which the people may desire to retain. However, there could be many good arguments advanced for placing these two sections in a new state constitution to the exclusion of all detailed provisions which might be inserted.

The State Constitution

Article I.

Section 1.

The Legislature shall establish,
maintain,
organize,
and provide for the support of
a liberal system of education,
throughout the State.

The educational institutions established
by the Legislature
shall be open,
without fee or charge, to
all residents of the State
under such conditions as the
chief state administrative body
for the control and regulation
of the schools shall direct.

Section 2.

The appropriation of or the
use of public funds,
directly or indirectly,
in aid of any person, or persons,
corporation,
school, or other institution
shall be prohibited,
unless such are
owned or controlled exclusively by the
State or
a political subdivision thereof.

The suggested constitutional provisions are to be noted for what they omit to regulate. The positive provisions need little discussion. The first section places the duty upon the state to establish, maintain, organize, and provide for the support of a liberal system of education throughout the state. There are no handicaps imposed by stating the definite types of schools to be organized, ages of pupils, or how the support is to be provided. In other words, the legislature may establish any school or schools it may desire, spend funds in any way it may direct, and raise the funds in any way it finds advisable. The provision is mandatory that schools must be maintained throughout the state.

The second part of *Section 1* intends to make the schools free of charge to all who are to benefit thereby. It seems that in a democracy the making of schools of equal quality available to all is but one step towards providing that basic equality. One state (Alabama) still has on its statute books a provision (*Sec. 182, School Code 1927*) which allows a school board to collect an incidental fee from each and every student for the purpose of providing repairs, improvements of grounds, and other incidental expenses. This provision was upheld in the courts as late as 1926.[47]

Section 2 provides for the use of public funds only in public institutions. Thirty-four of the states now have provisions which prohibit any aid to sectarian schools. It is a fundamental principle of educational administration and organization that the schools be publicly controlled and managed and in our country this principle does not seem to be seriously questioned. At least, it is so firmly established, that it can put such a provision into the constitution so that any change in this particular could not be made except after thorough discussion and action by the people. This section will also prohibit expenditures in aid of telegraph lines, railroads, and public corporations each of which has called for a constitutional prohibition in several of the states.

There are other matters which are commonly placed in the constitutions of the states which relate to control of expenditures. One concerns the debt limit. Twenty-six states now have constitutional limitations as to the amount of local indebtedness which may be incurred. These limits vary from 2 per cent to 10 per cent of the assessed value of the local property.[48] Scientific information and data as to the amount of indebtedness which it is possible for any given fiscal unit to assume, and within what limits fiscal units of any given wealth may most wisely assume indebtedness are still unavailable. A related question to those mentioned above, and one about which we have still less data, is that of determining what proportion of the total indebtedness of any given fiscal unit should be allotted for

[47] Kennedy *v.* County Board of Education, 214 Ala. 341, 107 So. 907.

[48] Anderson, Wm., *American City Government*, p. 589.

school purposes. In these days of rapidly changing conditions, it is certain that no such provisions should be placed in the constitution of any state,[49] and it is debatable as to whether or not there should be a statute which places limitations upon these matters. One of the authorities on the subject of Municipal Government, in a most thorough summary of this important topic, advocates that there be no constitutional or statutory limits upon indebtedness and that the matter be left to some administrative agency.[50]

[49] Lutz, H. L., *Public Finance*, p. 609.

[50] Anderson, Wm., *American City Government*, p. 591.

CHAPTER III

ADMINISTRATIVE VERSUS LEGISLATIVE CONTROL

The following topics will be discussed in this chapter:

I. Criteria for determining the proper province of administrative control.

II. Advantages of administrative over legislative control.

III. Bases for determining what control shall be exercised by the state and what left to local government.

IV. Types of administrative organizations developed in principal countries.

V. Bases for determining division of powers between central and local administrative units of the educational organization.

I. Criteria for Determining Whether a Matter Is to Be Regulated by Statute or Left to Administrative Action

Until recently no one had formulated any definite criteria for determining when the regulation of a matter should be left to administrative action. Dr. Freund, of the University of Chicago Law School,[1] however, in a most thorough comparative study developed certain criteria for determining the proper provinces of statutory and administrative regulation.

The criteria which Freund developed for determining the proper province of administrative power paraphrased and illustrated briefly are:

1. Administrative authorities should be delegated power to regulate those matters the nature of which makes it difficult to distinguish the lawful from the unlawful. In this class of matters it is recognized that legislative control is legitimate, but its use is attended with peril or liable to abuse. Administrative bodies should be granted control under general statutory regulations to administer such matters.

[1] Freund, Ernst, *Administrative Powers Over Persons and Property*, p. 28.

Illustrations:

The administration of contracts, compromises thereon, the undertakings in supplementary contracts, and the exact determination of the discretion of a board in letting contracts after bids are matters falling in this category.

2. Administrative bodies should regulate those matters for which there are no determined and definite standards. The legislature should not attempt to define by statute those matters for which it is unable to establish definite standards for the guidance of the people who are to execute them.

Illustrations:

This may be illustrated many times by the varied experiences with a school expenditure program. Definite and scientific standards are not available for the guidance of the legislatures. Recent research has contributed much to various problems, but it has just made a beginning. Who knows what should be the exact and necessary cost for the education of a pupil in any particular grade of any type of a school? What supplies and equipment are the desirable standard for any particular type of classroom? What are the data which should be placed in a financial report in any particular school district? What are the steps in the audit of school expenditures?

3. Administrative regulation may be desirable and necessary to determine compliance with statutory laws. Laws will not enforce themselves and, therefore, some administrative authority must be granted and charged with such supervisory powers as will insure knowledge and method of enforcement. It serves as an advance check upon the legality of action.

Illustrations:

How is the State to know that the money is being expended for the purposes intended, except by administrative supervision of budgeting and accounting? The same type of supervision is necessary to insure the wise expenditure of funds, as well as enforce compliance with the laws regulating the borrowing of money.

4. Administrative regulation is proper where liberty of private action is desired. Minimum standards set up by legislative mandate many times tend to become maximum standards. In a democracy it is desired that each unit develop the highest type of school possible. Minutiae of statutory regulation oftentimes are severe hindrances to individual initiative.

Illustrations:

How could the junior high schools have been developed, if statutes had allowed only an 8–4 organization? Is the establishment and maintenance of a school camp an expenditure for educational purposes? Is the teaching of adults to play bridge or to dancè a proper expenditure of public funds for educational purposes?

II. Advantages of Administrative Over Legislative Control

Freund, in another and earlier treatise said:

> Legislative power can . . . be exercized more effectually and more in accordance with the spirit of the constitution through delegation than directly. This consideration should weigh against abstract theories regarding non-delegatibility of legislative power.[2]

Goodnow, another most thorough student of and authority on administrative law, and particularly interested in its application to municipal government, said:

> The experience of the Western World would seem to prove that administrative rather than legislative control is the kind which will secure the desired results.[3]

A trend from statutory to administrative regulation is noted in England by Sir Josiah Stamp, who, in commenting upon "Recent Tendencies Towards the Devolution of Legislative Functions,"[4] states five reasons why the legislatures are delegating more power to administrative bodies. Stated briefly these reasons are:

1. Legislatures do not like to deal with conditions where the variety and detail of circumstances are so great and so little obvious to the legislator that he does not desire to deal with them.
2. Many problems have answers known only as society develops and therefore the legislator keeps away from such matters.
3. Matters may be so technical that only experts can deal with them.
4. Many matters cannot await legislative action and therefore power to regulate must be left to administrative officers.
5. All political parties desire smooth administration, and, therefore, do not desire to make details of the administration matters of party strife.

On page 55, Sir Josiah Stamp makes the following significant statement:

---

[2] Freund, Ernst, *Standards of American Legislation*, p. 302.

[3] Goodnow, F. J., *Municipal Government*, p. 381.

[4] Stamp, Sir Josiah, *Current Problems in Current Finance*, Ch. II.

No act of Parliament, today, can, on the surface of it, legislate in precise terms for the application of its principles to every person and case, to whom, or to which it may apply. That is quite impossible; and, with the modern pressure upon legislation, it is becoming even more impossible.

That the delegation of legislative power to an administrative body has legal sanction is stated by Chief Justice Taft:

The maxim that a legislature may not delegate power has some qualifications, as in the creation of municipalities, and also in the creation of administrative boards. . . . The latter qualification is made necessary in order that the legislative power may be effectually exercised. In creating such an administrative agency, the legislative power must enjoin upon it a certain course of procedure and certain rules of decision in the performance of its function. It is a wholesome and necessary principle that such an agency must pursue the procedure and rules enjoined and show a substantial compliance therewith to give validity to its action.[5]

This evidence and reasoning leads to the conclusion that the state has the power to create administrative boards or officers to direct the educational affairs of the state. The advantages and the reasons why administration is generally gaining power at the expense of both the legislatures and the courts have been pointed out. The Inter-State Commerce Commission, the Radio Commission, the United States Treasury Department, in the Federal government, and the Workmen's Compensation Boards, and the Public Utilities Commissions in each of the various states are each administrative bodies which are daily exercising legislative, executive, and judicial powers.

Attention is called to the fact that the school organizations have not grown apace with this development in other fields. It is true that state education departments here and there have exercised very great powers, but always with reference to very specific matters which have been relatively few in number. The growth of such powers has been sporadic rather than steady.

Apply the criteria developed by Freund, and it is easy to determine why our school codes have not been more effective. The lawmakers have tried to regulate by statute, after brief legislative study, matters for which school administration has not evolved any definite standards. A law written without definite standards is many times simply a sore spot to which various legislative "salves" are applied until finally one is discovered which, at least for the time being, appears to heal the sore.

[5] Witchita, R. R. *v.* Public Utilities Commission, 260 U. S. 48, 43, Sup. Ct. 51.

One of the contributions which this study seeks to make is to call attention of educational leaders to the fact that statutory legislation is but one means of regulating and controlling school administration. In days of rapid growth, changes in ideals concerning educational matters and the consequent lack of standards tend to make strict and inflexible legislation a rather dangerous instrument in regulating all types of school administration. Our Congress never even attempted to regulate radio by legislation, it at once created by law a Radio Commission and, realizing its inability to keep pace with the rapid developments in this field, left the matter to the Commission. Congress recognized the lack of standards and the dangers of inflexibility. Some of the recent educational developments have not been any less rapid in growth. Yet educators, in the great majority of cases, seek to solve many of their problems by legislative rather than administrative control.

The law has had a long and steady growth. It is extremely conservative. It usually lags behind social progress. The courts want to be certain that the people want what they have sought to have enacted into law.

The solution of our school administrative problems, however, cannot be solved in a simple and direct manner. The whole control cannot be turned over to administrative authorities. No such panacea exists. The legislature must erect safeguards (see page 39) and there must be certain types of administrative organization developed and perfected before it can be assured that any great improvement will come. The safeguarding and insuring of the proper functioning of the machinery set up is another important problem to which this investigation is directed.

The problem, from a governmental point of view, is a very difficult one to answer. The application of the evidence discussed heretofore in this study will certainly tend to limit detailed legislation and place the power of control in administrative bodies. The task is to allocate this power as between central and local authorities. What powers shall be given to the state department of public instruction and what shall be given to local administrative bodies? To find suggested answers to this most difficult problem, studies in the field of political theory must be consulted.

III. State Versus Local Administrative Control

Bases for determining what control shall be exercised by the state and what left to local government.

As has been discovered in the study of the legal power of the state over school expenditures, the state may go practically as far as it likes in regulating expenditures. It is not, therefore, a question of legal power; the state's power is practically absolute. It is a more serious question when it comes to a consideration of the extent to which this absolute power is to be exercised. This is really a most fundamental problem in political science. It is especially important in the particular phase of the law discussed herein, as the power which controls the purse may, through that power, control many other things.

This problem has not elicited from students of politics many clear-cut statements of policy. Much has been written but there still is a scarcity of definite evidence and criteria to guide the legal student through this complex situation. The difficulty is that the fundamentals rest upon the underlying philosophy of government in which one has faith. Even though agreeing to such a philosophy, the adherents quite frequently again diverge when it comes to a practical application of any theory of government.

Twenty-five to thirty years ago there were several graduate students of Columbia University who attempted to study the effects of certain centralizing tendencies in certain American states.[6] One of the principal topics discussed by each of these investigators was that of the effect of the centralizing influence upon the administration of schools. Each pointed to an assumption of power by the state over the school system. Rawles cited evidence of the good effects in Indiana and, to prove his point, used several of the measures later used by Ayres in his Index. Orth shows the steady and gradual growth of the central authority in Ohio. Whitten concludes that in Massachusetts the central authorities had about reached the place where there was no need of further central control, and prophesies that the equalizing of the burden of school support may lead to further centralization. These four dissertations are the most thorough studies we have of the effects of such centralization a quarter of a century ago. These men who observed strong centralizing tendencies in education then would, no doubt, be amazed at the present status. These theses offer an opportunity for other careful students to

[6] Whitten, R. H., *Public Administration in Massachusetts, The Relation of Central to Local Authority* (1903); Orth, S. P., *The Centralization of Administration in Ohio* (1903); Rawles, W. A., *Centralizing Tendencies in theAdministration of Indiana* (1903); Fairlie, G. A., *The Centralization of Administration in New York State* (1898).

study the conditions in these states today, and out of such studies some measures might be devised to show objectively the results of some administrative practices which will furnish us with better criteria for the evaluation of central control in school administration. This study cannot begin to go into this fascinating subject. The practical problem involved is to secure that proper balance of expert advice, supervision, and experience of central authority and at the same time secure the advantages due to the initiative, resourcefulness, and liberty possible under local action. Both are necessary for the proper development of our institutions.

IV. Central Control Over Local Affairs

Types of Control

Types of administrative organizations developed in the principal countries.

Sidney Webb, in his book *Grants in Aid* (published in 1911 and revised in 1920), sets forth in the light of his own and another study[7] the three principal types of relations between central and local governments developed in the leading countries of the western world.

> If we look over the world of highly developed nations today, we may recognize three main types of relation between local and central governments:
>
> (1) Bureaucratic-Continental-France-Germany-Belgium-Austria, etc. . . . we find local administration entrusted in the main to salaried officials, often of special training and high professional qualifications, who are sometimes actually appointed by, and whose work is, at any rate, closely supervised by, and completely subordinated to the various central departments of the Executive Government.
>
> (2) At the other extreme stands the organization of local government in the United States, where the cities and the towns are, broadly speaking, autonomous corporations. . . . This, which has its merits, as well as its characteristic drawbacks, may be termed the Anarchy of Local Autonomy. . . . It has been said, with some exaggerations, but with more truth than patriotic Americans usually realize, to have given the United States, at least in many great areas, the worst local government of any country claiming to be civilized.
>
> (3) In the United Kingdom we have, by characteristic good luck, stumbled on a third arrangement. John Stuart Mill drew pointed attention to the fact that the central executive department could hardly fail to have at their command a wider experience and a greater knowledge than any

[7] Grice, J. Watson, *National and Local Finance* (1910).

> local body could possess. . . . What we had to find was some way of securing national inspection and audit, and the amount of national supervision and control that was required in the interest of the community as a whole, without offending the susceptibilities of local autonomy, and without losing the very real advantage of local initiative and freedom to experiment. Without theory, without science, and, indeed, almost without the notice of political students, a solution has been found in the device Grants in Aid. The National Government in the course of the three-fourths of a century from 1832 successively "bought" the right of inspection, audit and supervision, initiative, criticism and control, in respect of one local service after another, by the grant of annual subventions from the National Exchequer in aid of the local finances, and, therefore, in relief of the local taxpayer . . . created a new species of administrative hierarchy, which has attributes of its own, and which, with our particular kind of local government, produces results in a remarkable combination of liberty and efficiency.[8]

Webb's study is a most complete, historical, and analytical summary of the principal plans of local and central administrative relationship. This brief summary may—and a full study of the original manuscript cannot fail to—call attention to the inherent possibilities for control through our own state aid policies. The manner in which we are ultimately to influence educational policies through state aid is a matter which should be of profound import to students of educational administration. Note that Webb said that this policy of control following "grants in aid" followed unconsciously and unnoticed by students even of political theory of the era in which it was developing.

The fundamental problem for American administrators is not whether or not there will be central control over the schools through control of income and expenditure; the real question is how that control is to be exercised in establishing educational policies. We are now engaged in large state aid equalization programs in several of the states. Different in many ways from the English conception, nevertheless these are "grants in aid" given for the direct purpose of accomplishing certain definite objects.

It is only good business sense and sound governmental policy to see that money aid accomplishes the purposes for which it has been provided. The state must see it through its many ramifications, and trace the ultimate good it does to the children of the state and thus to the upbuilding of the state itself. This means

[8] Webb, Sidney, *Grants in Aid*, pp. 4–6 (1920 ed.).

supervision, inspection, suggestion, and, in the case of non-compliance, the strong arm of the state administration to enforce the policies. A state committed to a policy of attempting to establish equality of educational opportunity cannot for a moment relax its vigilance. It cannot permit any unit no matter how small or how large to squander its own or the state's funds. A state establishing such a policy must exercise control. If the education of every child within the state is the concern of the state, then the state must see to it that every child secures the training which will benefit him and society. Those communities which furnish such opportunities will need but little of the state's supervision; those with but little educational leadership will require a large amount of control and supervision. The state cannot stand by and see a single school district abnegate its rights, or refuse to do its duty. It must, and will, find some means of controlling such situations should they arise.

Webb points to many inconsistencies, "shortcomings," and problems connected with the English Grants in Aid. Our form of government will not support in either theory or practice the Continental Bureaucratic system. There are many indications that we are not satisfied with our own "Anarchy of Local Autonomy."

V. Relation Between Central and Local Units in School Administration

Bases for determining division of powers between central and local administrative units of the educational organization.

Our most careful and thorough student of educational administration from the legal and historical points of view has been Cubberley. In his latest book on *State School Administration*, Cubberley treats this whole matter in a very thorough manner. He points out certain definite standards of action and sets up some criteria. In common with the writers on political theory he has failed to set up standards which might be universally applied. Perhaps it cannot be done. Let us examine some of Cubberley's writings:

> While our conceptions as to what powers and duties can be advantageously entrusted to local administration units are changing with time, there is, nevertheless, a certain demarcation between the powers and duties of communities which ought to be observed in all educational legislation and state administra-

tive control. This line of demarcation will vary somewhat in the different states, according to the degree of educational progress already made, the peculiar genius of their institutions, the types of subordinate administrative units involved, and the amount of money available for administrative work, but the line nevertheless exists in all of our states. Up to a certain point oversight and control are very desirable: too much liberty may easily mean inefficiency and waste.[9]

Unity in essentials, and large liberty to communities in the matter of non-essentials; as high minimum standards for all as is possible; constant stimulation of the local subdivisions to exceed the minima required; large local liberty in the choice of methods and tools and the extension of work; the protection of state standards from being lowered by private agencies; the freeing of the larger and more progressive communities from a uniformity perhaps necessary for small and more backward communities . . . these ought to be essential features in any wise state educational policy.[10]

In all such matters as the methods of bookkeeping and accounting, uniform fiscal years, and uniform fiscal returns, the State should prescribe such a degree of uniformity as will produce intelligent and comparable records. In all such matters as the kind or kinds of school which must be provided, the minimum length of school term which must be maintained, the general nature of instruction required to be given, standards for the certification of teachers, school supervision to be required, sanitary standards to be maintained, equipment to be provided, minimum rates and forms of taxation to be imposed, minimum salaries to be paid . . . it is essentially the duty and business of the State to determine the minimum standards which should be permitted, perhaps classifying communities into groups and requiring different minima from each, but always leaving to any given community the right to exceed these minima if it desires to do so.[11]

Cubberley has stated in as concise and definite language as possible this elusive problem of the proper division of powers as between the central and local governments when applied to school administration. The philosophy and detailed application, as stated by Cubberley, will be followed in this study, in the main, in the separation of the powers of administration as between the state and its local units.

---

[9] Cubberley, E. P., *State School Administration*, p. 298.

[10] *Ibid.*, p. 300.

[11] *Ibid.*, pp. 314–15.

CHAPTER IV

STATE CONTROL OF LOCAL SCHOOL FINANCIAL ADMINISTRATION

POWERS GRANTED TO THE STATE BOARD OF EDUCATION AND TO THE STATE COMMISSIONER OF EDUCATION

The provisions of the code as proposed and the underlying principles of law are discussed under the following headings:

I. The legislature does not have authority to delegate its power to make a law, but it may delegate power to an administrative body to determine facts and to act in accordance with principles and regulations which the legislature has established.

II. The legislature has been held to have the right to establish the purposes and policies for which expenditures shall be made by the local school districts.

III. Powers delegated by the legislature to a State Board of Education or to the State Commissioner of Education must be very definitely safeguarded.

IV. The proposed code provisions are justified in the light of legal principle and the need of such regulations as urged by authorities in school administration.

V. The power of the State Commissioner of Education to exercise certain judicial powers has been upheld in the states which have definitely delegated such power to him.

THE LEGAL POWER TO DELEGATE LEGISLATIVE POWER

I. The legislature does not have authority to delegate its power to make a law, but it may delegate power to an administrative body to determine facts and to act in accordance with principles and regulations which the legislature has established.

The following authorities establish this principle:

The legislature cannot delegate its power to make a law; but it can make a law to delegate a power to determine some fact or state of things upon which the law makes or intends to make its own action depend.[1]

I cannot see why, on general principle, powers that can be delegated to administrative officers of a municipality for exercise within a municipality are

[1] Gray, J. M., *Limitations of Taxing Power*, sec. 540.

not equally the subject of delegation to state administrative officers for exercise throughout the state.[2]

The state may confer upon the governing boards such authority as it shall deem wise, but subject to alteration at all times, and to be taken away at the discretion of the state.[3]

The same theory is upheld in cases cited to show that the school district is but an instrument of the state,[4] and other support of this principle of conferring authority will be discussed in a consideration of the delegation of the judicial power to the State Commissioner of Education.[5] There is, therefore, no question but that this type of authority may be delegated to the State Board of Education in the absence of any constitutional limitation.

The Legislature's Power to Direct the Purposes and the Policies of School Expenditures

II. The legislature has been held to have the right to establish the purposes and policies for which expenditures shall be made by the local school districts.

The power is retained by the state to approve expenditures of certain types. The right to approve the plans for new buildings is exercised in sixteen states,[6] and building sites by four states (Indiana, Maryland, South Dakota, and Virginia). To the list given by Reeder, state supervision of plans is required by Delaware, Georgia, Idaho, Iowa, New Jersey, North Carolina, Pennsylvania, and South Carolina. These states either have a code regulating the erection of buildings or designate some person in the department of education to exercise such control. In Vermont and New Hampshire the State Board of Health passes upon the plans for the purpose of insuring proper sanitation. In Massachusetts the State Supervisor of Plans has to approve all school building plans.

The State Superintendent is empowered in Arkansas and Kansas to set up standards for maps, charts, globes, and school apparatus. As long as states keep the local district organization, this plan might be wisely extended. Local school boards are in many cases rather susceptible to sales talks, and how a state can expect boards to select wisely such materials without professional

[2] Village Saratoga Springs *v.* Saratoga Gas Co., 191 N. Y. 123 (1908).

[3] Rawson *v.* Spencer, 113 Mass. 40 (1873). [4] *Ante*, p. 10ff. [5] *Post*, p. 42ff.

[6] Reeder, Ward G., *The Chief State School Official*, p. 46. Ala., Ky., La., Me., Md., Mich., Minn., Mont., N. Y., N. C., N. D., Okla., S. D., Utah, Va., and Wis.

advice is difficult to comprehend. It might be a forward-looking policy for the National Education Association to set up a Bureau of Standards where definite tests would be made of many materials used in schools, and reports issued thereon for the benefit of state departments and through them to the local districts. In this field there is an opportunity for some real contributions in the field of testing and administration.

One very debatable form of control is that of requiring all the schools in a state to use an absolutely uniform state adopted series of textbooks. Tidwell [7] reports that twenty-five states have state-adopted textbooks. Only sixteen states, however, have complete adoption, as in nine states the requirement is for elementary texts alone. Nothing could be more inflexible, in so far as educational procedure is affected, than the requirements of many of these laws. Tidwell advocates for Florida a multiple list of books, from which the local district may select the books it is to use. This type of control is an establishment of standards, yet leaves to the local district liberty to select its textbook from among several books, any one of which meet a reasonable minimum standard. The rigid requirement of the use of one series, as is all too prevalent among the states, is an illustration of dictatorial establishment of policies and procedure. This difference in state policy is well worth keeping in mind.

An illustration of the extreme differences in educational policy followed in this matter of textbook adoption, which in effect demands an expenditure of funds for articles beyond the control of the local boards, is found by an examination of the constitutional provisions of the states. The constitutions of California and Oklahoma provide that local schools must use the state-adopted texts, while Colorado and Wyoming absolutely prohibit by constitutional mandate any legislative action which would mean state-wide adoption of texts. The fact is pointed out that both sets of states cannot be right as to policy. It seems that such matters might well be left to administrative action, so that any adoptions could be made after a consideration of the needs and educational policies of the state.

The regulation of the local affairs of a school district has gone on steadily, until today statutory enactment regulates the length of terms, the salaries paid teachers, the textbooks which must be

[7] Tidwell, C. J., *State Control of Textbooks*, p. 6.

used, teachers' qualifications, libraries, laboratory equipment, and various other sundry items. The requirement that the local school district must meet such standards is, in effect, a mandatory establishment of an educational policy and an indirect control of the purposes of expenditure. These state standards must be met before any other expenditures are made, or the local district will run the risk of losing the state aid to which it is entitled. An examination of the statutes shows that at least thirty-five states make some such requirement. This indirect control of expenditures leaves in some states less than 10 per cent of the money which the local district can expend without consulting some state standard, rule, regulation, or code.

Students of education do not have any great objection to most of the standards mentioned above. The principal question is concerned with the nature and extent of such dictation. Certainly no one can object to the establishment of minimum standards in these matters, but there should always be opportunity for exercising individual initiative, and the further care taken that local districts are encouraged to go far beyond the minimum. There is also the necessary provision that the local units shall have their voices heard in the establishing of the standards.

Power to Withhold Funds

Seventeen states [8] provide definitely for the withholding of funds from local districts for violation of various regulations of the state department. Very few cases, however, have gotten into the courts. This may be taken as some evidence either of laxity on the part of the state departments or of fairness in the administration of the funds. It would be interesting to know the real reason. A recent New Jersey case upheld the right to withhold funds in order to enforce a ruling of the state department.[9]

The withholding of state aid from a school district is a most illogical penalty to place upon a school district. The state as a sovereign power has the right and the duty to provide for the education of its people. It seeks to require schools to come up to certain standards. It then withholds from these same schools the funds which are in most cases probably necessary to put the

[8] Reeder, Ward G., *The Chief State School Officer*, p. 52. Cal., Ill., Ind., Md., Mass., Minn., Mo., N. Y., N. J., Okla., Pa., R. I., S. C., Tex., Utah, S. D., and Wis.

[9] Board of Education West Answell Township *v.* State Board of Education, N. J. L., 135 A. 664 (1927).

requirements into effect. What is wanted is positive action on the part of the school boards and not the taking away of educational opportunities from the children of the community. It seems as if other means should be provided to regulate our financial affairs in so far as state supervision is necessary to secure the use of state aid for the purposes for which it was given. The code herein proposed will make other provisions for the enforcement of state policies.[10]

Safeguards to Be Observed in Delegation of Administrative Power

III. Powers delegated by the legislature to a State Board of Education or to the State Commissioner of Education must be very definitely safeguarded.

The state department of education cannot be entrusted with such large powers of control except that the grant of the power is definitely and surely safeguarded.

One of the foremost English authorities upon government, Dr. Cecil T. Carr,[11] has formulated five criteria for safeguarding the delegation of administrative power. Stated briefly these criteria are:

1. Delegation should be only to a trustworthy authority which commands the public confidence.
2. The limits within which the delegated power is to be exercised ought to be definitely laid down.
3. The safeguard of interested advice. This is the case where action cannot be taken until advice has been, at any rate, heard and until certain bodies presumed to be affected or to have expert knowledge have been consulted.
4. The safeguard of public notice. If the price of liberty is eternal vigilance, then the public ought to be always reading notices. Carr believes that general notice will be watched by interested groups.
5. The final safeguard is the machinery for revocation or amendment.

These criteria have been kept in mind in developing the suggested plan of state control of the financial administration [12] and will be used in delegating power to local administrative officers and bodies. It was not the purpose of this study to go into the details of the type of administrative body to be established by the state. Certainly before any such broad powers as those herein

[10] Appendix A, Proposed Code, Art. IV, sec. 6, and Art. V, sec. 1, subdiv. 6.

[11] Carr, Cecil T., *Delegated Legislation*, pp. 27ff.

[12] See Appendix A, Proposed Code, Arts. IV and V.

are delegated to a state board of education or to a state commissioner of education, such bodies and officers must have a high professional status. Such bodies must be able to command the respect of the people of the state or it would be useless and dangerous to give them the powers suggested. The standards which should be followed in the organization of the state administrative organization are discussed, defined, and evaluated by Schrammel.[13] It is only to such a body as Schrammel suggests that these powers should be delegated, thus meeting Carr's criterion 1. The limits of the powers to be conferred are as definitely limited as is possible and still insure the liberty and flexibility of action which is desired. The length and definite enumeration of powers is a result of meeting criterion 2.[14] Section two definitely provides for interested advice as well as the safeguard of public notice, criteria 3 and 4. Finally section five definitely provides for revocation and amendment which satisfies criterion 5.

These code provisions also meet another criterion which might be applied to any delegation of power. The Supreme Court enunciated the following doctrine over fifty years ago:

> The theory of our government, state and national, is opposed to the deposit of unlimited power anywhere. The executive and the judicial branches of these governments are all of limited and defined powers.[15]

A system of checks is to be noted upon every administrative body or person, but always with the plan in mind of allowing the greatest freedom of individual action and liberty consistent with the public interest.

Justification of Provisions of Proposed Code [16]

IV. The proposed code provisions are justified in the light of legal principle and the need of such regulations as judged by authorities in school administration.

Section 1. This section is intended to give the State Board of Education a real standing in so far as the law is concerned. The law tends in most states to interpret rather strictly the powers given the administrative officers. Legislative declarations of this type are sometimes of great value. Such a declaration of policy

[13] Schrammel, H. E., *State Educational Organization*, pp. 91ff.

[14] References are to Proposed Code, Art. IV, Appendix A.

[15] Loan Association *v.* Topeka, 20 Wallace U. S. 655 (1874).

[16] References are to sections noted of the Proposed Code, Art. IV. See Appendix A.

may be of aid to the courts in more liberally interpreting the powers granted to the State Board of Education.

Section 2. This is a definite enumeration of the powers which a state board of education should have which, in any way, would control the purposes and policies of expenditure. This list has been checked with the powers which Cubberley advocates in his book on *State School Administration.* Cubberley mentions all the items except *d*, *i*, and *j* which are included by this investigator because the results of this study indicate that they should be included in view of the fact that local units have been unable to handle these matters successfully.

Section 3. The provisions of this section will enable the state board of education to manage the state aid funds in accordance with general policies as enumerated by the statute. State aid can be administered for the most part in a rather mechanical manner, but even under the best plan there are instances where administrative discretion is needed to insure real educational opportunity.

Section 4. The provisions of section 4 are an attempt of this investigator to provide for the *criteria 3 and 4* set up as safeguards by Dr. Carr for control of administrative action, namely interested advice and public notice. If our democratic form of government is to be improved, does it not seem that the profession of teaching must be among the first to put into effect and practice some of the most important principles of public action? It might be possible for the school people to develop a form of coöperation which might greatly improve our forms of governmental action. It is further hoped that the working out of such a plan of action will promote a greater spirit of real research in the administration of school affairs generally. Autocratic control by the state authorities would not be successful under such a plan. The public press and a modicum of courage on the part of the school people would tend to make state authorities formulate all policies on the basis of the best authority the state possesses.

Section 5. This provision is in many states superfluous. The common law is already formulated in a rule practically as stated in this section. Its inclusion is justified on the ground that it will remove any doubt from the minds of the courts, the legislature, and the people. It will also serve as a warning to the state administrative body that if it does not exercise in a democratic and efficient manner the powers and duties granted it, such power may be taken from it.

Section 6. In order to make the power of the state board of education effective, it must have power to enforce its commands. The penalties are developed in accordance with the theories of punishment which have been applied to other penalties in this proposed code and discussed on page 131.

Since the same arguments and reasoning are equally applicable to the office of the State Commissioner of Education as are applicable to the organization of the State Department of Education, no special justification is needed to give the Commissioner the power to execute the policies of the State Board of Education. Under Article V, Sec. 1, he has no powers to act except as the executive authority of the state board. A different problem confronts us, however, when we consider the powers granted in section 2 of Article V which will be presented fully in the next division of this study.

The State Commissioner's Judicial Powers [17]

V. The power of the State Commissioner of Education to exercise certain judicial powers has been upheld in the states which have definitely delegated such power to him.

These sections (2 and 3) of Article V of the proposed code regulating the judicial power of the State Commissioner are adapted largely from the New York Education Law upon this matter. The New York Law has been very successful in taking out of the courts many matters which ordinarily and justly would be matters of court action. This New York Law has been tested for over one hundred years as to constitutionality and the extent of the powers granted herein. Most of this division (Article V) of the proposed code has been thoroughly tried out in the courts of New York State. An excellent study of the history and present status of the Commissioner's power in this state has been recently made by Brubacher.[18]

Brubacher concludes:

> . . . there is apparently one advantage in the growth of the commissioner's judicial power which will be permanent, namely, the administration of the education laws by a tribunal technically expert in the field of education.

[17] All references are to Art. V, Proposed Code, Appendix A.

[18] Brubacher, J. S., *The Judicial Power of the New York State Commissioner of Education.*

To the great extension of public welfare legislation and to the increasingly minute specialization in human pursuits, there seems no other answer but a degree of judicial specialization.

Another reason for giving the judicial power over such ministerial and judicial matters and cited by Brubacher is a statement made by Draper, one of New York's able Commissioners of Education.

There is a different relation between the Commissioner of Education and a proceeding before him than that which obtains between a court and a proceeding before it. A court is disinterested in all questions except the facts and the law. The Commissioner of Education is the administrative or supervisory officer of the educational system of the State. He is bound to have an interest in the equity, right, and justice of all questions having a bearing upon the administration of the educational system. He must determine judicial questions with a view to the general effect upon the school system as well as to the technical requirements of the law.[19]

The status of the law in regard to giving to administrative officials the power to hear appeals has received attention from legal authorities. Cuthbert Pound of the New York Court of Appeals says:

The entire subject of Administrative Law and procedure is in a comparatively undeveloped stage. . . . A strong desire to impair the finality of the decisions of administrative boards may be reflected in future legislation providing for a wider range of judicial review, or conceivably, on the other hand, constitutions may be so amended as to create a body of law, outside the fields of the courts of justice, to be administered by officials without judicial review.[20]

This entire field of the law has been recently reviewed by Dean Albertsworth of the Wyoming Law School.

The conclusiveness of administrative findings must be conditioned on a procedure which is consistent with due process of law. . . . Somewhere along the line, a hearing of some kind must have been given before a party's rights or liabilities are affected. This hearing must include opportunity to present evidence and to inspect that of the opponent.

It must appear always that the administrative body had power to act and that its findings were free from fraud or bias.

The extent of the judicial review will depend often upon the nature of the interests dealt with.[21]

---

[19] Election of Member of Board of Education, Union Free School District No. 6, Judicial Decisions 175, 183 (1905).

[20] Pound, Cuthbert W., *The Growth of American Administrative Law*, p. 130.

[21] Albertsworth, E. F., in *Harvard Law Review*, 35: 127.

As this procedure is a comparatively new development of the law, it may be worthy of much greater use than has been made of it in the past. There should be no desire on the part of the state education departments to set up courts of their own. However, where the matters are concerned with details (not rights), discretion (not fraud or illegality), it appears that a logical development of the law would lead to the placing of finality of certain decisions upon certain administrative authorities within the field of education.

The states of New York, New Jersey, Iowa, and Texas have allowed their chief executive officer the most power in this particular. Rather limited power over certain matters, such as the right of a teacher to appeal for redress in various matters, is allowed in several states. Dr. Brubacher makes the following statement concerning these appeals and their effect:

> Some significance also attaches to the fact that most states allow "appeals" to the education department. An appeal is preferable to an action at common law. In an appeal, the education department can dispose of all phases of a case in a single decision. If the case be one involving discretion, then an appeal will invoke that very discretion in the appellate tribunal in the very same manner and to the same extent that it was possessed originally. It cannot only reverse a wrong action, but it can direct the appropriate one so as to afford redress to all persons who have been injuriously affected. An action at common law insures only to the benefit of the person who brings it and gives only pecuniary knowledge, without substituting a correct procedure in place of an erroneous one.[22]

It should be remembered that in accordance with the principles of constitutional law, the Commissioner will be permitted to exercise only those powers directly and specifically given to him and no others. He must also act in the manner prescribed and no other manner.[23] This is an extremely important point. Many legal authorities are strongly advocating this type of procedure. Brubacher concludes that the courts will be favorable to its development.

> But whatever the statutory provision or the judicial precedent, it is well to remember that the courts will be in no hurry to overrule the decisions of the state education department. Indeed, the courts are inclined to give great weight to the constructions put on statutes by administrative officers charged with their enforcement and execution.[24]

---

[22] Brubacher, J. S., "Judicial Powers of State Commissioners of Education," *American School Board Journal*, December, 1928, p. 35.

[23] Board of Education *v.* Tuttle, 211 N. Y. S. 423 (1925).

[24] Brubacher cites in support of his contention: Bullock *v.* Cooley, 225 N. Y. 566; and People *v.* Finley, 211 N. Y. 51.

It will be necessary to examine some cases to discover just how this power has operated. A few cases have been selected from those states which have given rather large powers to the state department to direct matters of school administration upon appeal. The cases selected have to do with control over expenditures.

The legislature of New York has given the State Commissioner some tremendous powers with reference to actually directing expenditures. The power of the Commissioner has been upheld so far as to permit him actually to levy a tax to pay a debt involved in the payment of tuition due another district.

> The Commissioner directs that the claim be paid by the trustee of school district No. 4 and, in case there are no moneys at present available for this purpose, to immediately raise by tax . . . such sum as shall be necessary to pay said claim with interest. This is not a diversion of a fund in existence or maintained for common school purposes, but is a levy of a tax pursuant to law authorizing it to be levied.[25]

During the same year, however, the power was denied when applied to the transportation of pupils in a certain type of school district. This case was decided upon other grounds than that of the power of the State Commissioner of Education to levy a tax, but the dicta of Judges Kellogg and McCann enunciates an opinion decidedly adverse to any such assumption of authority.

> Indeed, he was not elected by the people of the State or by the elected representatives of the people. If he may impose local taxation, an exception heretofore unknown in the law will have been made, and a striking example of taxation without representation will be permitted to take place. There can be no doubt that the Commissioner's order, which of necessity will result in the laying of taxes and in terms provided therefore, is a taxing order. In my judgment, the legislature was without authority to confer upon the Commissioner the power to make the order in question, even if the order is within the statute.[26]

The law, therefore, is that in New York, the State Commissioner may even force a local district to levy taxes to pay tuition; but such a power has rather dubious standing when applied to other purposes. This power of allowing the State Commissioner to force a local community to levy a tax to raise funds to enforce the orders of the Commissioner represents about the most extreme instance of liberal construction of such an officer's power. It is rather doubtful law. The fact that the Tuttle case was decided

---

[25] Board of Education Oneida *v.* Tuttle, 211 N. Y. S. 413, 125 Misc. Rep. 230 (1925).

[26] In re: Board of Education Brookhaven, 210 N. Y. S. 439 (1925).

by a four to three vote and that the court in the Brookhaven case went out of its way to deliver a lecture on such a matter shows that a lawyer in New York would have an excellent chance to enjoin any such action on the part of the Commissioner. Such an attorney would have on his side the weight of opinion in many other jurisdictions. This matter of the non-delegation of the power to tax is discussed at length, pages 86–89. This code does not seek to give the State Commissioner any such doubtful powers.

The Commissioner of Education in New York was denied the power to regulate the crediting of appropriations of state money given to the City of New York under state aid grant.[27]

In Texas where the State Superintendent is also given considerable power, he was granted "full power over the administration of school laws and business relating to the public schools."[28] The Texas State Superintendent may direct the payment of salary to a particular teacher,[29] but may not decide as to whether or not funds are being misapplied.[30]

The State Commissioner of Education in Tennessee is required to go into court and recover for the school district moneys unlawfully paid out.[31] Michigan also requires the State Superintendent to go into the courts in order to prevent unlawful and wasteful dissipation of school money.[32]

In New York, where a long line of precedents have upheld the Commissioner's power, there need be no fear of abuse of the power to decide numerous matters upon appeal.

> This delegated power of the Commissioner is not, however, general and unlimited. In order to oust the courts of their normal jurisdiction, it is not enough that the schools or the school system are more or less involved; in all matters outside its general policy, administration, and control, where the educational system conflicts or interferes with the rights and interests of the people, in the absence of express statute to the contrary, the courts retain and will exercise full jurisdiction.[33]

There is one device of control which has not been developed very highly in the United States. This is the device of public inquiry. England has found that an inquiry into local matters

[27] People *ex. rel.* Hylan *v.* Finegan, N. Y. 125, N. E. 97 (1919).
[28] Johnson *et al.* *v.* City of Dallas, Tex., 291 S. W. 972 (1927).
[29] Powell *v.* Matthews, Tex. Civ. App. 280, S. W. 903 (1926).
[30] Dallas *v.* Mosely, Tex. 286, S. W. 497 (1926).
[31] State *v.* True, Tenn., 95 S. W. 1028 (1906).
[32] Johnson *v.* Gibson, 240 Mich. 515, 215 N. W. 333 (1927).
[33] Miller *v.* Gould, 121 N. Y. Misc. 270 (1923).

and the publishing of the results will many times shame local districts into compliance with the regulations of the central authorities.[34] A code provision (Article V, sec. 4) is inserted in this proposed code to provide for this type of inquiry, if any state should desire to put such a practice into effect.

It is believed that the proposed code (Articles IV and V) will accomplish the following desirable ends: (1) increase efficiency by allowing greater flexibility of regulation and action; (2) avoid much litigation which now gets into the courts; and (3) secure expert knowledge and administration. The safeguards set up should tend to keep the state from becoming too autocratic, and should tend to greater coöperation between local and central government which is a very potent means of ultimately settling difficult questions.

---

[34] Ashly, Percy, *Local and Central Government*, p. 346.

CHAPTER V

ADMINISTRATION OF THE EXPENDITURE BUDGET

Principles of Administration and Points of Law Involved in the Administration of the Expenditure Budget

The following points will be discussed in this chapter in elaboration of Article VI of the proposed code provisions: [1]

I. There is general agreement among authorities that the preparation of the budget is an executive function.

II. There is a difference of opinion as to whether the expenditure budget should be on the "segregated" or "allotment" plan. The trend, however, in legislation in so far as it concerns schools is toward the "segregated" plan.

III. The encouragement of intelligent public participation in financial planning is an essential part of a democratic form of government.

IV. The courts and authorities in the fields of Education, Municipal Government, and Public Administration are agreed that public money should be expended in accordance with a well-prepared and well-considered plan.

V. The weight of authority as expressed in the court decisions is that public money must be used for the purposes appropriated.

VI. Statutes which prohibit the expenditure of funds without an appropriation having been made are interpreted very strictly.

VII. Statutory provisions prohibiting the expenditure of public money in excess of the appropriations will usually be strictly enforced.

VIII. The courts are in conflict as to whether money may be transferred from one fund to another.

IX. The courts will not allow statutory provisions to be violated or liberally interpreted, even though unforeseen emergencies arise.

X. Statutory provisions directing that contracts when made become encumbrances upon the appropriation will be upheld by the courts.

[1] Proposed Code to be found in Appendix A. See Art. VI.

XI. In the absence of statutory provisions the calendar year is a fiscal year.

XII. The decisions of the courts with reference to various problems concerned with the borrowing of money are in a state of confusion.

XIII. Neither the courts nor the legislatures have discovered any certain means of prohibiting deficits in expenditures for public schools.

XIV. In the absence of statutory provisions, there is no general rule as to the use to which a school board may put surplus funds.

Educational research has contributed several notable studies in this field of control of income and the preparation and adoption of the budget. The present writer has no desire to go over the ground so well covered by others. This study will simply cite the evidence of the findings by leading workers in this field. An adequate treatment of the entire evidence would be a recital of the material which may be studied at first hand and which is fairly well known to workers who are interested.

The problem of this dissertation is primarily concerned with the legal control exercised over the execution of the expenditure plan. Since, however, this is primarily a legal study, it is found necessary to go into certain of the legal implications of control of income a little more carefully. It is also necessary to give unity and completeness to the study, even at the risk of becoming prolix, to include the origin of the expenditure plan, in order to develop a complete code for the control of expenditures.

Preparation of the Expenditure Budget Is an Executive Function

I. There is general agreement among authorities that the preparation of the budget is an executive function.

There is little serious objection to the superintendent[2] of schools being designated as the official who is to prepare the budget of expenditures. Writers and students in this field are numerous who say in no uncertain terms that the superintendent should be the officer who is to prepare the budget, among them being Twente,[3] Engelhardt and Engelhardt,[4] Moehlman,[5] and Morris-

[2] See Proposed Code, Art. VI, sec. 1.

[3] Twente, J. W., *Budgetary Procedure*, p. 132.

[4] Engelhardt, N. L. and Engelhardt, Fred, *Public School Business Administration*. p. 519.

[5] Moehlman, A. B., *Public School Finance*, p. 176.

son.[6] Authorities in the fields of city, state, and national administration are practically unanimous in advocating strong executive leadership in the preparation of the budget. Buck [7] advocated a strong executive leadership in making our Federal Budget. Stourm,[8] the noted French writer on this subject, declares the preparation of the budget to be an executive function. The budget in Great Britain is formulated by the executive.[9] The Model Municipal Budget,[10] just formulated (1928) by a committee of authorities upon municipal administration provides definitely for the preparation of the budget by the executive.

The only objection which has been discovered in print to the superintendent acting as the chief budget officer comes from the school business officials.[11], [12]

The actual practice seems to support the contention for executive leadership in budget making. Emerson [13] found that in 215 cities, 92, or 43 per cent, of the superintendents actually made out the budget estimates and that the superintendent had a joint responsibility in 60 other cities, while the clerk or secretary prepared it in 30 cities and the board itself in 15. Buck [14] reports that "a majority of the states and the larger cities have the executive type of plan."

However, relatively few states have placed the responsibility for the preparation of the budget upon the superintendent of schools by statute. Emerson in 1925 reported Alabama as the only state directly giving this authority to the city and county superintendents of schools. At the present time Alabama, North Carolina, Utah, and Virginia give the power to prepare the budget to the city or division superintendent, the board of education keeping the final power of approval. The fact that three states, since 1925, have decided to delegate this power to the super-

[6] Morrison, J. C., *Legal Status of the City School Superintendent*, p. 150.

[7] Buck, A. E., *The Development of the Budget Idea in the United States*, p. 35.

[8] Stourm, René, *The Budget*, p. 3.

[9] Willoughby, W. W., *The System of Financial Administration in Great Britain*, p. 271ff.

[10] "Model Budget Law, National Municipal League," Supplement to *National Municipal Review*, Vol. XVII, No. 7, sec. 6, p. 441.

[11] Dick, Wm., *Proceedings*, 7th Annual Meeting Public School Business Officials, Rochester, 1918, pp. 7–13.

[12] Keough, W. T., "School Board Organization in Larger Cities," *American School Board Journal*, 1922, pp. 39–40.

[13] Emerson Wallace, "School Budget and Budget Procedure," *American School Board Journal*, 71: 51, July, 1925.

[14] Buck, A. E., "The Development of the Budget Idea in the United States," *Annals, American Academy of Political and Social Science*, 113: 31–39.

intendent of schools is important evidence of the trend of thought in the legislatures.

In Tennessee the county superintendent and county chairman have the responsibility for the preparation of the county budget for schools, while in Illinois the superintendent is supposed to furnish the board with certain information concerning the financial program. In Arizona the county superintendent presents the budget direct to the board of supervisors which must levy the amount requested. This is the only state which gives an administrative officer this immense power.

The details concerning the preparation, form, contents, divisions, etc., of the budget estimate of expenditures are kept at a minimum in the code herein suggested. As stated earlier in this discussion, the exact details of regulating the details of the budget for any given unit should be left to the supervision of the state commissioner of education.[15] If the state officials will take a coöperative attitude, give the benefit of their advice to the larger cities, and perhaps work out a plan for each group of organization units which have similar problems, it is felt that budget procedure may be greatly improved. The state will reserve the right, under this code, to demand a certain procedure if necessary, but the theory of many authorities in this field is that greater ultimate progress will be made in the former manner.

Since the fiscal year begins on July 1, the budget should be adopted before the year begins; therefore June 1 is placed as the date when the official machinery will commence to function. One month should be sufficient for the most animated discussion and expert consideration of the proposed policies involved in the expenditure program.

"Segregated" Versus "Allotment" Type of Budget

II. There is a difference of opinion as to whether the expenditure budget should be on the "segregated" or "allotment" plan. The trend, however, in legislation in so far as it concerns schools is toward the "segregated" plan.

The only item which will provoke a discussion of a real principle in the remainder of the section concerns the detail with which the budget shall be presented. This code provides it shall be in detail [16] but leaves the exact promulgation of the extent of

[15] See Proposed Code, Art. IV, sec. 2, subdiv. g.

[16] See Proposed Code, Art. VI, sec. 1.

detail to the state administrative authorities to work out with each city, but this plan does, by the insertion of the word "detail," contemplate a detailed budget. Among experts in the general field of budget making, there is a sharp division of opinion as to whether the "segregated" or "allotment" form of budget should be adopted. The earlier students on this subject as it relates to municipal administration were wholeheartedly in favor of the "segregated" budget.[17] Later writers in municipal administration have leaned toward the allotment idea, and the new Model Municipal Budget Law provides for the allotment principle.[18]

Educational authorities are inclined toward the "segregated" principle.[19, 20, 21] Emerson[22] in 1925 found thirteen states[23] which prescribed an itemized budget. An examination of the statutes (1927) shows that five additional states have provided for an itemized or segregated budget, namely, New Mexico, Rhode Island, Virginia, Utah, and Washington. Emerson also had seven states which required an itemized budget but which did not prescribe the form. These states were Arizona, Colorado, Connecticut, Massachusetts, Montana, New Hampshire and Pennsylvania, and to this list, since Emerson's study, Nebraska and Wyoming have been added. This represents a real trend toward definiteness in expenditure programs.

The statutes in Iowa, Michigan, Kentucky, Louisiana, and Maine permit the local district to determine the form of itemization. All of these states except Maine have voluntarily established uniform itemization through regulation by the state departments of public instruction.[24] There are, therefore, at the present time, 32 states which really prescribe in some form or another an itemized, detailed or "segregated" budget.

A difference in the administration of expenditures of municipalities from that of the schools is evident upon a close examination of the facts. It may be that these differences account for the

---

[17] Buck, A. E., "The Development of the Budget Idea in the United States," *Annals, American Academy of Political and Social Science*, 113: 31–39.

[18] "Model Municipal Budget Law," *National Municipal Review*, 1928, p. 443.

[19] Moehlman, A. B., *Public School Finance*, p. 176.

[20] Engelhardt and Engelhardt, *Public School Business Administration*, p. 528.

[21] Slater, C. P. and Greene, H. A., *Administration of the School Budget*, p. 24.

[22] Emerson, Wallace, "School Budgets and Budget Procedure," *American School Board Journal*, 70: 55, June, 1925.

[23] Ala., Calif., Del., Md., Nev., N. J., N. Y., N. C., Ohio, Okla., Ore., Tenn., W. Va.

[24] Emerson, *op. cit.*

prevalence of the "allotment" idea among the municipal experts. Cities quite often are engaged in immense business enterprises. Some cities own and operate utilities, the income and cost of which are quite often subject to wide fluctuations. A change in the cost of coal may cause large gains or deficits within a very short time. Public utilities are dependent to some extent upon weather conditions, business conditions, and many other factors which may make it impossible to estimate the costs or the revenues with any great accuracy. A difference of a few inches in the snowfall in any city makes a large proportionate difference in the expenses of that division of the city. Other types of weather conditions may greatly increase the cost of street maintenance.

On the other hand, the expenses for schools for any given fiscal period are fairly constant. The principal items of expenditures are for salaries of teachers, janitors, and supervisory officers. These salaries will take up from 70 to 90 per cent of the total budget for current expenses. As these salaries are fixed in advance they can be definitely figured. The cost of capital outlay is definitely known and the cost of debt service may usually be quite accurately forecast in the light of past experience. Maintenance charges are usually outlined fairly definitely in advance, as a certain number of buildings will be decorated each year, and the cost of this can be definitely estimated. In the main, the expenditures for schools can be estimated fairly accurately.

The segregated or detailed budget offers a real guide for the expending officers and may be used as a control of expenditures to the degree to which the expending officers are made to adhere to the expenditure plan.

It would be useless here to rebut any claims that the cities are wisely administering their finances under the allotment plan. Reports are made with frequent regularity as to the waste of public money by these governing bodies from all parts of the country —padded payrolls, excessive contract costs, extras allowed contractors, and other items of unwise expenditure. A recent indictment was given the cities by Will Durant.[25] It has just been discovered that the Chicago Sanitary Commission has been carrying on its payrolls nearly 1,000 employees who never pretended to do any work. The segregated budget might be abused under similar circumstances, but with state administrative control it is quite

[25] Durant, Will, "Has Democracy Broken Down?" *Forum*, Vol. 81, No. 1, January, 1929.

unlikely that such unwise or illegal expenditures would go on indefinitely.[26]

Participation of the Public in Budget Planning

III. The encouragement of intelligent public participation in financial planning is an essential part of a democratic form of government.

Section 2 of the proposed code is included to make possible increased participation of the people in the adoption of the policies of schools and to provide for popular control over the expenditure program. Many have written voluminously in support of the principle of popular control of a financial program, but few have attempted to work out a plan which would make for increased and more intelligent public participation. In the administration of the schools, executives have, as a rule, been afraid of the possible stress of such participation. If we believe in our form of government, the theory would indicate that control should begin and end with the people. The people's money is being expended and therefore they should have both a direct and an indirect control of the purposes for which money is to be expended.

Historically, the New England town meeting provided for a real and direct control of all matters of common interest. Due to changes in population and the complexity of our governmental machinery, it became impossible to conduct a public town meeting. Students of government have not devised the necessary methods to retain some of the great values of this type of public hearing. It has, therefore, been rather unfortunate from this point of view to note the present lack of public participation in public affairs. The agitation and adoption by several of our states of the initiative, referendum and recall is an attempt to regain some of this lost ground. It is true that in many New England towns the electors still meet and vote upon the school budget directly. In Arkansas, Idaho, Indiana, Kansas, New York, and Missouri, in the rural districts, the voters meet, propose, and adopt the budget. In Maine towns, Minnesota common school districts, Nebraska and Oregon rural school districts only, in Connecticut and New Jersey small districts, Michigan townships, and in Wyoming, the voters have to approve the amount to be expended.

[26] *New York Herald Tribune*, November 28, 1928, p. 2.

As the powers of the boards of education have developed, the fact that it was the people's money that was being expended was forgotten in many places. Utah is the only state which provides by statute for a public hearing upon the budget. In Nevada the voters may by petition demand a vote upon the tax levy. The people, by statutory law, have retained the power in most of the states to approve issues of bonds for new buildings and excess tax levies.

Our present difficulty as to fiscal dependence upon city councils, fiscal courts, and other fiscal bodies represents an abortive attempt to impose checks upon boards of education. It is the argument of this investigator that the placing of such indirect control in the hands of other governmental or extra-governmental agencies tends to remove the power of control farther from the people. One of the recent developments of the survey movement is that Strayer and Engelhardt are presenting the recommendations of the surveys which they make directly to the people. If such a technique works in such cases, it would seem to have considerable merit in our governmental affairs. Dr. Strayer in a public address made at the meeting of the Department of Superintendence (Cleveland, February 25, 1929) said:

> . . . that provision, which enables the people to record their judgment with regard to the program developed and the cost involved, is essentially sound.

This plan will call, however, for better techniques in the preparation of our plan of expenditures. Such plans would have to be gotten up in such shape that the so-called average citizen can understand what it is all about. Understandable budget data placed in the hands of the individual citizens should draw from the citizenship many constructive suggestions. The ideas of the public would have a real influence upon board action. As for the superintendent who is charged with the duty of preparing the expenditure program, he will be sure that all expenditures which he includes are defensible before he presents them to public scrutiny. It will afford the superintendent a chance to exercise the highest type of school salesmanship.

This plan will further permit the people to express themselves, and to make their influence felt upon this one item of school administration. It will be a real chance to permit the people to express themselves definitely as to certain policies.

Judge Cooley attributed to Lord Bacon the following statement which calls attention to the difference between burdens imposed as compared with those freely assumed: "It may be all one to the purse, but it worketh diversely upon the courage."

Students of educational administration who have definitely expressed themselves as in favor of a public hearing upon a public hearing are Twente [27] and Clark.[28] The Model Municipal Budget Law provides for a public hearing,[29] and Buck [30] advocates open procedure by a responsible legislative body.

A recent judicial statement made concerning the value of such public hearings and increased participation by the public in budget matters is reported from New Jersey. Although this statement directly concerns the adoption of the city budget, the ideas are equally applicable in principle to a school expenditure budget.

> The act requires much publicity to be given the items in the budget, and provides for a hearing and final action upon the budget. Indeed, the purpose of the Budget Act is not only to secure greater uniformity in municipal financing, but to give the members of the public a better understanding of the financial condition and affairs of municipalities in which they are interested, and to place at the disposal of the governing bodies the data necessary for intelligent action on financial matters, and thereby safeguard the public interests.[31]

The board of education now has under this suggested code the superintendent's plan for the educational policies and their probable cost, the public reaction to this plan, and its own thought and counsel. The budget may be adopted at once if the board is clear as to its duty in the matter. If its duty is not clear, then, within the ten days provided after the public hearing, it should be able to gather such additional data as it may desire, weigh the arguments, and pass intelligently upon the budget. The superintendent may find that the time is not proper for the inauguration of certain of his policies. It may be a sign of strength rather than weakness should he decide that the public is not yet ready to accept certain far-reaching policies. It is much better to inaugurate a policy under the proper auspices, even though the policy may be delayed several years, than to "start something

[27] Twente, J. W., *Budgetary Procedure.*

[28] Clark, H. F., "Suggestions for Scoring School Budgets," *American School Board Journal,* 71: 47–48, October 1925.

[29] "Model Municipal Budget Law," *National Municipal League,* sec. 7, p. 442.

[30] Buck, A. E., "The Development of the Budget Idea," *Annals, American Academy of Political and Social Science,* 113: 31–39.

[31] Mackey *v.* Belvidere, N. J. L., 128 A. 859 (1925).

which cannot be finished." On the other hand, a public hearing offers the superintendent a chance to educate the public as to the policies he and his board are undertaking. His board may not be as progressive as he believes sound policy would demand. He has a chance through a public meeting to bring these facts to the surface without personal embarrassment. It may perhaps be urged that "cranks" and "faddists" will be hard to control. Perhaps these opposition forces may serve as desirable checks. Such persons will have to earnestly believe the thing they advocate, otherwise they will not be able to stand the effects of such "scorching" public opinion as is expressed in an open meeting in the United States today. A just cause has nothing to fear from the American people. "The best governments are always subject to be like the fairest crystals, wherein every icicle or grain is seen, which in a fouler stone is never perceived." The above quotation from Lord Bacon might well serve us as a guide in public administrative work.

It will be noted (Article VI, sec. 3) that the code provides for the placing of full responsibility upon board members who wish to make changes in the tentative budget submitted by the budget officer. The fact that a "yea" and "nay" vote is called for upon each item to be changed, will definitely place responsibility for any changes made necessary by the failure to budget and appropriate funds. This provision does not necessarily place a label of "contrariness" upon any member of the board who may wish to voice his disapproval and cast his vote and influence against any particular items in the budget. On the other hand, it furnishes an opportunity for the board to consider each item in relation to policy. Should any member not agree or approve of any policy, he is permitted to express his dissent upon that particular item of expenditure without voting against the entire budget plan. Each educational policy under this plan, if questioned, will have to be decided upon its own merits. This plan will also tend to prevent the advocate of particular "hobbies" securing an appropriation by attaching it as a rider to the budget and forcing it through because of the fact that other members of the board do not wish to jeopardize the entire financial program. The plan will also tend to make "log-rolling" increasingly difficult to accomplish.

In an itemized, wisely planned, and fully considered budget, the adoption of the expenditure budget (sec. 4) should make it the appropriation bill as well. The adoption of the expenditure budget should *ipso facto* make the appropriations for the items and amounts therein named.

Budget Appropriations as Controls of Expenditure

IV. The courts and authorities in the fields of Education, Municipal Government and Public Administration are agreed that public money should be expended in accordance with a well-prepared and well-considered plan.

It has long been the law and a fundamental principle of public finance that public money shall not be used except as provided by law. "No money shall be drawn from the Treasury but in consequence of appropriations made by law" is a much-quoted provision of our Federal Constitution.[32] Agger declares this to be a fundamental principle of all public finance.[33] Strayer and Haig [34] in the Educational Finance Inquiry say that it is of the greatest importance that "boards of education adopt budgets which limit their appropriations to their income and then confine their expenditures to the appropriations voted." From the ranks of the school business officials comes a statement of the importance of this principle.[35] The authorities in municipal budget making set this principle up as a standard of good financial practice,[36] as does the new Model Municipal Budget Law proposed by a committee of the National Municipal League.[37] This proposed law was formulated and adopted by a committee composed of a large number of leading authorities in municipal government and may be said to represent the agreement of municipal government authorities upon this most important matter. The code proposed absolutely prohibits an expenditure unless an appropriation is provided.[38]

School boards are able to keep within their budgets if they so desire. Smith found that all but three of the twenty-five cities of over 30,000 population which he studied had been able to keep within the budget. Smith concludes by saying:

---

[32] Constitution of the United States, Art. I, sec. 9, par. 7.

[33] Agger, Eugene, *The Budget in the American Commonwealth*, pp. 20–25.

[34] Strayer, George D. and Haig, R. M., *Educational Finance Inquiry*, Vol. I, p. 187.

[35] Brackett, H., "Developing a Segregated School Budget," *Proceedings of Public School Business Officials*, Philadelphia Meeting, May 1926, p. 47.

[36] Upson, L. D. and Rightor, C. E., "Standards of Financial Practice," Supplement, *National Municipal Review*, Vol. XVII, No. 2, par. 9.

[37] Model Municipal Budget Law, National Municipal League, sec. 12.

[38] See Proposed Code, Art. VI, sec. 5.

In other words, cities of both types so handle their finances that there is little necessity for exceeding their appropriations.[39]

Even in business the claim is made that a budget can and must be followed:

A recognition that when a budget is adopted it constitutes a financial program that can and should be followed. No man will keep within budget limitations unless he believes this can and should be done and it is surprising how much an operating man can squeeze within the limits of a budget allowance, if he believes that those budget limits can and should be followed.[40]

Total Expenditures Must Be Kept Within Estimated Income

That a board of education should keep its total appropriations within the estimated expendable income is such a fundamental and elementary principle of finance as not to require citation of authority from the fields of municipal finance or from the general field of public finance. There is not a single writer who has ventured the opinion that the rule should be otherwise. Boards of education in the past, however, have not followed this principle and many of them have accumulated large floating debts. It is therefore imperative that a statutory provision (sec. 5) be made to cover this elementary financial principle.

Funds Must be Used for the Purposes Appropriated

V. The weight of authority as expressed in the court decisions is that public money must be used for the purposes appropriated.

General Status of School Funds

School funds are in the nature of trust funds and do not belong to the district or to the officers of the district, but to the public.[41]

The above statement should be kept in mind in considering the whole matter of the administration of school funds. The board of education is dealing with public funds, not their own, and the legal barriers which have been erected are for the protection of the public money. Since the money originated with and always belongs to the public, the people should have the ultimate and determining voice in its expenditure.

Under our form of government, this power of expenditure is

[39] Smith, H. P., *Business Administration of a City School System*, p. 30.

[40] Fernald, H. B., *Certified Public Accountant*, 7: 108, April 1927.

[41] Andrew *v.* Stuart Savings Bank, 204 Iowa 570, 215 N. W. 807 (1927).

delegated to the board of education. The courts appear to be of the opinion that when a board of education makes a spending plan, it should not depart fundamentally from the plan and outline of policies proposed. Because of the fact that this phase of the law has not been emphasized in other studies, the law is quoted somewhat in detail.

A case of some standing which directly concerns the character of school funds is reported from California.

> . . . The school moneys never lose their character of public moneys belonging to the state and are to remain under the control of its officers for the purposes for which they have been appropriated. The fact that they have been appropriated to the several school districts does not give to those districts any proprietary right therein, or any right to their custody, but the districts through their authorized agents have the right merely to contract for their proper disbursement within the purposes authorized by law.[42]

The most clear-cut cases of appropriations for one purpose being diverted and used for other purposes comes in those cases involving building expenditures. Usually the funds for buildings are raised in a special way and are quite often administered separately from the general or current expense fund. Therefore the issues are more easily followed than in some other classes of cases. One of the strongest statements is reported from Florida.[43]

> Funds in the control of a board of public instruction, which were raised by the public for the specific purpose of building a school house, constitute trust funds for that purpose, and may not be diverted to any other purpose until the purpose for which such funds were raised has been accomplished.

The New Jersey Supreme Court (1916) would not allow the transfer and use of a surplus in the building fund for the repair of other buildings.[44]

In Louisiana, the Orleans Parish School Board attempted to pay janitors' wages out of the funds raised for "maintenance, construction and repair" of buildings, but the court decided that janitor's work is not maintenance under the ordinary interpretation of the word.[45]

Ordinarily school boards do not plan their expenditures for buildings so as to have surplus funds available and so the question

---

[42] Kennedy *v.* Miller, 97 Cal. 429, 32 P. 558 (1893).

[43] Miami Bank and Trust Co., *v.* Board of Education, Brower Co. (Fla.), 80 So. 307 (1918).

[44] Heston *v.* State Board of Education *et al.*, N. J., 98 A. 305.

[45] Orleans Parish School Board *v.* Murphy, 156 La. 268, 101 So. 268 (1924).

more likely to arise is whether or not general or special funds raised for other purposes may be used for buildings. Here we have a conflict of authority. The courts, however, have usually been rather liberal in allowing the use of current funds for building purposes. In Wisconsin [46] there is a statutory provision which prohibits maintenance and operation funds being diverted for the building of schoolhouses. This provision was strictly interpreted by the Supreme Court in 1927.[47]

In Kansas [48] the "Teacher's Fund" was comingled with the "Building Fund" and the Court forbade the use of the "Teacher's Fund" for building purposes. The same principle involved was upheld in Utah [49] and Illinois.[50] The Pennsylvania Courts have said that the matter is one of discretion which each individual board of education will have to decide for itself.[51]

In Lincoln, Nebraska,[52] the board paid $113,306 from the current expense fund toward the erection of three school buildings, the total cost of which was $359,860. The Court stated that it could see no reason why this was not legal. Chief Justice Sharp of the Oklahoma Supreme Court [53] held that the board could apply the additional revenue available from the gross production oil tax towards the building of a new school. In California under a statute which provides for the erection of school buildings either with funds from a "bond issue" or "special tax levy," the court held it was legal to purchase electrical fixtures for a school building out of current funds. The court limited its decision by stating that the board could "raise small funds rather than resort to either a bond issue or a special tax levy as the cost of either would be greater than the bill for fixtures." [54]

A district in North Dakota overlevied taxes for teachers' salaries and transferred the surplus to the general fund for the purpose of ultimately securing enough funds to erect a building.[55] The court upheld this plan of creating a building fund.

---

[46] Statutes 1925, sec. 40.25 and sec. 40.26.

[47] Reisen *v.* School District No. 4 of Shorewood, 192 Wis. 283, 212 N. W. 783.

[48] Consolidated School District No. 6 *v.* Shawhan, Kansas City, A. 273 S. W. 182.

[49] Utah Ass'n Credit Men *v.* Board of Education Millard Co., 54 Utah 135, 179 P. 975 (1919).

[50] Kuykendall *v.* Hughey, 224 Ill. App. 550 (1922).

[51] Duff *v.* School District Perry Twp., 281 Pa. 87, 126 A. 202 (1924).

[52] Gaddis *v.* School District Lincoln, Neb., 139 N. W. 280 (1912).

[53] Board of Education *v.* Corey, Okla., 163 P. 949 (1917).

[54] Posz *v.* Taylor, Co. Treas., 61 Cal. A 523, 215 P. 107 (1923).

[55] Stimson *v.* Thorsen, N. D. 2 N. W. 351 (1916).

Status of Expenditures Made Without Prior Appropriations

VI. Statutes, which prohibit the expenditure of funds without an appropriation having been made, are interpreted very strictly.

It has been uniformly held that a contract made without an appropriation to pay the debt is void.[56]

The Massachusetts courts have recently decided (1928) that a seller of textbooks to a board of education cannot collect for the same if no estimate for such purpose has been made. The court said:

> The school committee is required, by Sec. 49 of Statutes 1914, c. 687, to submit in January of each year an estimate of the amount of money necessary for proper maintenance of the schools during the succeeding financial year; it is thus required to plan for its expenditures in advance. Obviously the legislative purpose cannot be accomplished if any department is allowed to make expenditures which were not included in the estimate submitted by it.[57]

The State of Oklahoma has a series of cases upholding the principle that there shall not be any contract or expenditure without an appropriation. As the statute is now interpreted, it is impossible even to contract with teachers for the next school year, prior to the adoption of the budget for the next fiscal year.[58] The legislature had definitely attempted to permit teachers to be hired prior to the beginning of the fiscal year but the statute [59] was declared unconstitutional.[60] As the annual school budget cannot be approved by the excise board prior to July first, this works an extreme hardship upon the teaching staff and supervisory officers.

A recent Indiana case, June 1928, makes a distinction between general and special appropriation administration which may offer some basis for permitting differences in application of this principle. Judge Nichols said:

> There are general appropriations such as are made by acts of the legislature and annually at regular meetings of city councils, county councils, and advisory boards. Such appropriations are necessarily prospective and in anticipation of revenues to be produced by taxation then provided for. The case relied upon by the appellee concerns such general appropriations and is not in

[56] Railroad School Township *v.* First State Bank, 73 Ind. 358, 126 N. E. 342 (1920).

[57] Parkhurst *v.* City of Revere, Mass., 161 N. E. 599.

[58] Gentis *v.* Hunt, *et al.*, 121 Okla. 71, 247 P. 358 (1925).

[59] Statute, sec. 10367, Oklahoma Statutes, 1921.

[60] School District 76 Creek Co. *v.* Bath, 102 Okla. 204, 250 P. 1003 (1926).

point under the facts here involved. Here we have a special appropriation, not one included in the annual budget, but one growing out of an emergency. To make such an appropriation lawful, the fund must be in hand at the time it is made, and without lawful appropriation there cannot be a valid contract.[61]

Attempts to circumvent the law have, of course, been tried. One plan attempts to make contracts upon the partial payment plan. A West Virginia board of education attempted to repair some buildings and purchase some furniture with an understanding that the same were to be paid out of next years' funds. It was enjoined from paying the balance due under such an agreement.[62] In California, however, it was held legal for a board of education to contract for progressive work upon a school building and pay part out of one year's funds and part out of the funds of the succeeding year.[63]

It has been held in New York that an architect may be hired before funds are available for the erection of a school building.[64] The court argues in this case that the board of education could not present to the city an estimate as to the amount needed for the purpose of erecting the building, and that the employment of an architect was necessary in order to arrive at this figure. Upon this ground the court decided that the board had power to put this claim in the budget and raise funds with which to pay it. A Colorado court, however, would not permit the payment of an architect hired under similar circumstances.[65]

Status of Expenditures Made in Excess of Appropriations

VII. Statutory provisions prohibiting the expenditure of public money in excess of the appropriations will usually be strictly enforced.

One of the best statements of judicial opinion of the reasons why the courts have upheld the "pay as you go policy" principle was enunciated in 1894 by Judge Holt of West Virginia.

See Acts, 1881, p. 168, c. 15. It commands with a directness and brevity that has but one meaning: "You shall not incur now any debt to be paid out of school money of any subsequent year." The policy intended to be subserved by this command is the result of widespread observation and long, continued

[61] Union School Township *v.* Moon, Ind. 162 N. E. 3, 61.
[62] Shonk Land Co. *v.* Joachim *et al.*, 96 W. Va. 708, 123 S. E. 444 (1924).
[63] Posz *v.* Taylor, Co. Treas., 61 Cal. App. 523, 215 P. 107 (1923).
[64] People *v.* Board of Education of Utica, 190 N. Y. S. 798 (1921).
[65] Mountjoy & Frewen *v.* Cheyenne Co. School District, 78 Colo. 162, 240 P. 464 (1925).

experience. These taxes are the lifeblood of the school system, and the current taxes of each fiscal year are needed for the current expenses of each year, the taxes of the subsequent year for the current expenses of the subsequent year, and by no sort of circumlocutory shift or device shall they be trenched upon and used to pay the debt of any previous year's contracting. This is a vital part of the fiscal affairs of the school system commanding and obligatory upon those who deal and contract with the board as upon the board themselves; and not the one more than the other can plead ignorance of the law. Its hardship and inconvenience, in special cases, such as building new houses in the independent districts to meet the wants of enlarged and growing schools, have been for several years a subject of common observation and remark. Yet this sweeping command of the general statute has thus far never been qualified, or in the slightest relaxed, and when done, if at all, it is likely to be done with caution, guardedly, and with an eye to the danger of abuse. But we have to take the law as we find it, for the lawmaking powers have thus far set their faces against permitted school moneys to be used and spent in anticipation of their levy and collection.[66]

The above principle was upheld in West Virginia in 1920,[67] and a like policy was upheld by the Oklahoma courts in 1925, Judge Mason saying:

The intention and plain purpose of Sec. 26, Art. 10, of the Oklahoma Constitution, is to require school districts and other subdivisions of the state government to carry on their operations upon a "cash or pay as you go plan." The revenues of each year take care of the expenses of such year, and any liability sought to be incurred in excess of such current revenue in hand or legally levied is void, unless it be authorized by a vote of the people and within the limitations provided by that section. . . . This limitation on the funds derived from taxation has resulted in the placing of legal restraints upon the expenditure of such funds with the purpose of preventing extravagant expenditures, as well as the prevention of unjust and tyrannical action against the rights of private property. Property is never secure from the lawless grasp of the government, unless the means of existence of the government depend upon the voluntary grants of those who own the property.[68]

This principle has been upheld in Washington,[69] Pennsylvania,[70] Massachusetts,[71] New York,[72] and New Jersey.[73]

The statutory requirement, that any expenditure exceeding the annual income must be submitted to a vote of the people of the

[66] Shinn *v.* Board of Education, 38 W. Va., 497, 20 S. E. 604.
[67] Wysong *v.* Board of Education, 85 W. Va. 729, 102 S. E. 604.
[68] Gentis *v.* Hunt, 121 Okla. 71, 247 P. 358.
[69] Wolfe *v.* School District No. 2, Columbia Co., 58 Wash. 212 (1910).
[70] McKinnon *v.* Mertz, 225 Pa. 85.
[71] Parkhurst *v.* City of Revere, Mass., 161 N. E. 599 (1928).
[72] Pierce *v.* Board of Education, 211 N. Y. S. 788, 125 Misc. Rep. 589 (1925).
[73] Perkins *v.* Newark Board of Education, 161 F. 767 (1908).

school district and passed by a two-thirds vote, was upheld in Oklahoma.[74]

A statutory provision [75] in Wisconsin will not permit [76] the expenditure of more money than the electors have voted for the erection of a school building.

Oklahoma so strictly enforces this principle of "no expenditure in excess of appropriation" that teachers employed and a lumber bill contracted for after the estimate had been exhausted had to suffer the loss of wages and the price of the lumber, respectively, on the theory that persons contracting with a board of education are presumed to know the status of the appropriations.[77]

There have been some courts which under certain circumstances approved expenditures made in excess of appropriations. A Kansas court [78] permitted the board of education to use the current expense funds to supplement a bond issue for a new school building, and held valid a contract made in excess of the bond issue. Judge Bouldin of the Alabama Supreme Court (1925) allowed a board of education to pay the salaries, amounting to $15,000 in excess of appropriations, for the year and allowed them to pledge its revenues for the succeeding year to pay such claims.[79] In a New York City case [80] it was pleaded as a defense that the appropriation had been exhausted. The court held that a judgment must be paid. This case was then appealed to the Court of Appeals and upheld by a four to three vote of the court, but unfortunately no written opinion was given. As this case concerned the payment of a judgment rendered by a court of law, its authority is somewhat lessened if it should be used to uphold the general principle. Judge Finch in the decision of the lower court expressed a very strong dissenting opinion.

Transfers and Administration of Funds in General

VIII. The courts are in conflict as to whether money may be transferred from one fund to another.

A leading case upon the general principle of whether or not funds voted for a specific purpose may be used for another purpose

[74] Board of Education Oilton *v.* Short, Att'y General, 126 Okla. 70, 258 P. 915 (1926).

[75] Section 40.00, subdiv. 5, and sec. 40.26 subdiv. 1, Wisconsin Statutes 1917.

[76] O'Loughlin *v.* Dorm *et al.*, 168 Wisc. 205, 169 N. W. 572 (1918).

[77] Myers *v.* Ind. School District No. 1, Comance Co., 33 Okla. 257, 230 P. 498 (1924).

[78] Wright *v.* Board of Education Leavenworth, 106 Kan. 469, 188 P. 439 (1920).

[79] Heustess *v.* Hearin *et al.*, 213 Ala. 106, 104 So. 273.

[80] Clayton Construction Co. *v.* Craig, Comptroller, 204 N. Y. S. 619 (1924).

is that of the City of Hoboken *v.* Phinney in which the court held:

> Upon general principles of law, a fund raised for a specific purpose, and placed in the hands of an officer for such specific purpose cannot be lawfully applied to any other. Any such appropriation would be a violation of the trust and so contrary to law.[81]

Bond funds must be administered separately from maintenance funds.[82]

> Funds created and set apart for the support and maintenance of the independent or white schools of said independent school district cannot be expended and used for the support and maintenance of the separate or colored schools. . . . The converse, of course, is true.[83]

Kentucky[84] empowers the board of education to place all funds received in one common fund and to distribute this fund so as to provide an efficient system of schools.

Temporary Transfers

California Statutes quite definitely provide for transfers of funds (Sec. 1858, Political Code). The arguments of the court in a case concerning this statute are illuminating, and should receive weight in the consideration of a code regulating expenditures.

> In connection with what has been previously stated, it appears that a school district must annually carry over a surplus equal to 30 to 40 per cent of the amount of its yearly expenditure or pay interest for several months on a like amount unless the foregoing provisions of Sec. 1858 can be upheld. Under like circumstances, no private business would carry over an idle surplus of such magnitude in one fund or pay interest on its indebtedness, while it held an equal amount in other funds not immediately needed to pay demands against them. It would require cogent reasons to justify a court holding that the legislature is without power to provide that the business of the state shall be conducted upon businesslike principles.[85]

Where two districts are in the process of merging and the transfer of funds or of appropriations arises, it has been upheld that the merging of the funds temporarily is permissible.[86] [87]

---

[81] 29 N. J. L. 67.

[82] McPhail *v.* Tax Collector, Texas Cir. App. 280 S. W. 260 (1926).

[83] Board of Education of Sapulpa *v.* Board of Commissioners, 127 Okla. 132, 260 P. 22 (1927).

[84] Carroll's Ky. Statutes, sec. 4399, subsec. 7.

[85] Fawcett *v.* Ball, 80 Cal. App. 131, 251 P. 679 (1926).

[86] Krause *v.* Thompson, 138 Ark. 571, 211 S. W. 925 (1919).

[87] Ogunuit Village *v.* Inhabitants of Wells, 123 Me. 207, 122 A. 522 (1923).

Transfers of Appropriations Within the Budget or Estimate

Cases involving transfers of appropriations from one item or division of the budget to another item or division have only occasionally got into the courts. There are several reasons which may be advanced for this fact. In the first place, budget procedures are relatively new in our states. Baker [88] writing in 1916 said that so far as he had been able to learn Oregon was the only state which required the annual preparation and publication of a budget by every school board in the state. Few states have statutes definitely defining just what an estimate or budget shall consist of. Emerson [89] in a study made in 1925 found that only 14 states which required a budget from all school districts and cities prescribed at least the minimum of itemization. Secondly, citizens, unless definitely personally interested, are not likely to interfere with the administration of the board's finances so long as funds are not wasted. Thirdly, few people know what and when changes are made in the expenditure plan. Lastly, there are few states which have budget laws sufficiently strict as to prohibit transfers [90] or which require publicity and formal procedure in making the transfers.[91]

The habit of making transfers seems to have been extensively practiced in Buffalo in 1923.[92] The practice did not draw any condemnation from the court. Judge Thomas of the Kentucky Court of Appeals [93] registers the opinion that he sees no reason for sticking so close to the estimate made.

Transfers Not Permitted

Where the statutes have a provision prohibiting the transfer of appropriations from one division or item to another, such statute is rather strictly enforced. In the case cited,[94] the court would not allow money of the teacher's fund to be transferred to and used in the incidental fund.

---

[88] Baker, George M., in *American School Board Journal*, Vol. 53.
[89] Emerson, Wallace, in *American School Board Journal*, 70: 55, June 1925.
[90] Ala., Ark., Md., Mont., W. Va., Wis.
[91] Calif., Conn., Iowa, Ind., Mo., N. M., Pa., Ore., Tenn.
[92] Fleishmann *v.* Graves, 235 N. Y. 84, 138 N. E. 745.
[93] Gragg *v.* County Board of Education, Ky. 252 S. W. 137 (1923).
[94] Cleveland Village School District *v.* Zion, Kansas City App. 190 S. W. 955 (1916).

Transfers

The expenditure budget and appropriation plan must be definite and rigid enough to enforce policy control on the part of the people and the board, yet it must be for administrative purposes elastic enough to permit of solving the everyday financial problems of boards of education. If, after the adoption of the expenditure plan which is to represent the policies of the board of education for the next fiscal period, changes are desirable or necessary, such changes should be made. The method of making such a change is exceedingly important, however. It is a policy which is being changed and not simply an administrative adjustment to conditions. It is therefore provided in this plan to require exactly the same procedure as was required in the case of the adoption of the original policy. The people do not want their boards of education to be capricious and, therefore, necessary or desirable changes, although not impossible to make, should be surrounded with the same safeguards, with a chance for the public to state its views and also a chance to discover the exact position of each member of the board upon these important policies.

Minor changes in policy and elasticity of financial management are provided by allowing changes within each budget division. It is presumed that the budgets will be organized upon a functional basis and, therefore, changes within the division will not seriously affect policies. Such changes usually only involve administrative and discretionary details and need not be subject to the public hearing, but the power to make the changes must rest with the board as a check upon possible policy changing by administrative officers.

The principle of allowing transfers is upheld in general by Engelhardt and Engelhardt,[95] Buck, [96] and Reeder.[97]

The proposed code (Art. VI, sec. 9) allows transfers, but with certain restrictions. Any transfer from one division to another usually involves a change in policy and therefore has to be safeguarded the same as the original budget. It would be very easy for the board of education to adopt a very sound budget plan and by "juggling" the appropriations around completely change the

[95] Engelhardt and Engelhardt, *Public School Business Administration*, p. 553.

[96] Buck, A. E., *Budget Making*, pp. 219–21.

[97] Reeder, Ward G., "The New Budget Law in Ohio," *Research Bulletin*, Vol. V, No. 12, pp. 241–44.

adopted policies. Should a change in policy be necessary, it should be important enough to be worthy of a plea for public support. Transfers within the divisions of the budget usually do not change the policy or policies, but are matters largely of administrative convenience or necessity. Such changes may be made at any board meeting. It should be noted that only the board by official action can make any change in the budget plan as adopted.

Emergencies

IX. The courts will not allow statutory provisions to be violated or liberally interpreted, even though unforeseen emergencies arise.

Even the best financial plans are sometimes upset by emergencies. Floods, fires, epidemics, lawsuits, loss of funds, funds not up to estimate are things which cannot be foreseen. Since 1916, the value of the dollar has changed so much and so rapidly that many boards of education have found themselves in a difficult financial situation. In this day of rapid industrial growth there quite frequently arise situations where the rapid growth of school population outruns financial policies. How have the courts viewed such situations and how have the legislatures attempted to handle such emergency situations?

The City of Williamsburg, Kentucky, in 1926 wished to replace a building which had burned. The city could not build a suitable schoolhouse without exceeding the constitutional limitation as to debt. The constitutional limitation as to indebtedness reads that it must be adhered to "unless in case of emergency, the public health or safety should so require." Judge McCandless held that though the courts had held, under this clause, that while a public waterworks might be erected in excess of the constitutional debt limit, ". . . that the burning of a schoolhouse does not create an emergency which will validate a bond issue in excess of the 2 per cent limitation." [98]

The heavy increase in school population put a West Virginia district into debt. The facts were admitted that the buildings were out of repair and the congestion extreme. The court said:

> The crying need of rudimentary education for the children of the industrial workers in the shops and mines was recognized as a matter of public welfare,

[98] Nelson *v.* Board of Education, City of Williamsburg, 213 Ky. 714, 231 S. W. 808.

but as a matter of right. No doubt these matters influenced the state officers and the board in the formation of its budget for 1921–1922, when the indebtedness in excess of funds amounting to $84,190.18 was included. This situation and these considerations have appealed to us. Tersely stated, it is defense of justification on the ground of necessity arising from an unusual condition. However, arguments of necessity and inconvenience have little weight. Many governmental restrictions and limitations are found to be inconvenient and cannot be annulled on the ground of necessity.[99]

An interesting and novel procedure was attempted in Oklahoma to care for an emergency.[100] Under the law the excise board may make a supplementary appropriation to a school district in case of an emergency, provided the financial statement of the board of education shows an actual surplus of revenue in some fund. This board of education attempted to sell furniture and equipment and place the money ($15,057) in an account so as to show the necessary surplus. The court wisely prohibited such action on the grounds that if a board could sell equipment, it could sell buildings and sites to meet current expenses. By this process a school district would soon be without school grounds, buildings, or equipment.

An emergency was defined in New Jersey in 1925. The definition has not been questioned in any court since that date.

> The "emergency" contemplated is the statutory condition outlined by the legislature, and equivalent to a public calamity, resulting from fire, flood or like disaster, or by some unusual occurrence that could not by any provision of any local appropriating body be reasonably anticipated.[101]

It is in the light of this definition that an emergency is defined in this code.[102]

Unless the statute is very carefully drawn, school boards may be able to declare emergencies as existing when ordinary financing would attend to the needs of the district. An Indiana district declared an emergency to exist and voted a bond issue of $55,000 to pay for a building and architect's fees. The building had been completed and an emergency did exist in so far as the board had no plans for financing the building. However, the court held that the board should have financed the building first and then built it rather than the reverse, as it was practiced in this case.[103] Most

---

[99] Shonk Land Co. *v.* Joachim, 96 W. Va. 708, 123 S. E. 444 (1924).

[100] Threadgill *v.* Board of Education, City of Colgate, 85 Okla. 121, 204 P. 1100 (1922).

[101] Lyons *v.* City of Bayonne, 101 N. J. L. 455, 130 A. 14.

[102] Proposed Code, Art. VI, sec. 10.

[103] Union School Township *v.* Moon, Ind. 161 N. E. 714 (1928).

states require the boards of education to depend upon the ordinary borrowing power to care for emergencies. There is some evidence, however, that the legislatures are beginning to think more seriously of this problem. California, Ohio, Iowa, New Mexico, and Oregon request or allow boards of education to provide for an emergency or contingent fund in the budget. In Washington a unanimous vote of the board will allow any unappropriated money to be used in case of great need. Michigan, North Dakota, and Oklahoma provide that judgments shall be paid out of the next tax levy. In Indiana the Township Advisory Board may provide for unforeseen expenses and the County Commissioners may do the same in North Carolina.

Encumbrances Upon Appropriations

X. Statutory provisions directing that contracts when made become encumbrances upon the appropriation will be upheld by the courts.

Comparatively recent cases in a few jurisdictions make the lawful contracts, once they are entered into, legal encumbrances upon the funds appropriated for that purpose.[104]

Oklahoma has a statute which makes contracts legally entered into encumbrances upon the appropriation. This statute was upheld in Gentis *v.* Hunt, *supra*, with the following unqualified language:

> The total amount of such legal contract is always on hand and reserved until legally paid out in discharge of the obligations of the district under contract.

Even in the absence of a statute the courts are becoming somewhat impatient with poor business methods of school officials, as may be noted from the following opinion:[105]

> It is not presumed that public officers so inefficiently conduct the public business as to render it difficult or impracticable, on issues properly framed, to determine at any time the amount of outstanding obligations. Particularly in a case such as this, where the fund in question is limited to one specific use and claims against the fund must be based upon contracts, the terms of which as stated are presumptively within the knowledge of the auditor, it would be a simple matter to establish whether or not there were any outstanding claims.

---

[104] Doss *v.* O'Toole, W. Va. 92 S. E. 139 (1917); Utah Association Credit Men *v.* Board of Education, Millard Co., 54 Utah 135, 179 P. 975 (1919).

[105] Birch *v.* Monroe, 70 Cal. A. 656, 234 P. 125 (1925).

The State of New Jersey has an accounting system prescribed by the State Department of Public Instruction which provides that all outstanding contracts or obligations which are liquidated become at once charges against the funds to be charged therewith. The plan is claimed to be very effective.[106]

The Fiscal Year

XI. In the absence of statutory provisions the calendar year is the fiscal year.

One method of keeping expenditures within the estimated income is a clear and concise definition of the fiscal year. Most states and the national government provide that the fiscal year shall be from July 1 to June 30, of the following year. Some states make the calendar year the fiscal year for schools. It may be of interest to point out the fact that Ohio, one of the states which revised its finance laws in 1927, changed its fiscal school year from July to July to the calendar year basis. Where no definite statement is made in the statutes as to what constitutes the fiscal year, McQuillan says: "If no provision fixes the beginning and end of the fiscal year, the fiscal year means the calendar year." [107] This opinion is modified somewhat by a Kansas Court which held that the fiscal year was ". . . simply the year embraced in the annual term of the opening and closing of financial accounts." [108] The right of the legislature to fix the limits of the fiscal year for schools was upheld in Louisiana.[109]

In the case of borrowing money with a limitation upon the borrowing power based upon the fiscal year an interesting case developed in Kentucky. The fiscal year of the city and that of the school district are defined upon different bases. The school fiscal year was from July to July and that of the city from January to January. The court held that the school had to borrow its money on the basis of the school fiscal year and not that of the city.[110]

The closing of the fiscal year presents a real administrative problem to school officials. It is at this point that many errors may be covered up, deficits or surpluses concealed, or the accounts

[106] Close, Egbert, in *American School Board Journal*, 68: 58, 123, 127, March 1924.

[107] McQuillan, E., *Municipal Corporations*, Vol. V, p. 970, sec. 2335.

[108] Leavenworth National Bank *v.* Reilly, Kan. 156 P. 747 (1916).

[109] State *ex rel.* Day *v.* Rapides Parish School Board, 158 La. 249, 103 So. 757 (1925).

[110] Board of Education *v.* Newport, Ky. App. 224 S. W. 680 (1920).

so juggled as to make it appear that payments made during the close of one fiscal year are chargeable against the funds of the succeeding fiscal year, or *vice versa*. Other subterfuges might be used which would make all other forms of budgetary control useless. There is little information available upon this topic. Since we have no standards as to just how to regulate this matter which may be reduced to code provisions, under the second criterion suggested by Freund this becomes a matter for the State Administration to make such regulations as will accomplish the purpose. Perhaps experimentation of several different methods in several jurisdictions may evolve some method which will really control. Since these facts may be discovered through better accounting and auditing, these divisions of the state department may be able to contribute much toward its solution.

Provisions for the care of these matters are provided in Article VI, section 12 of the proposed code.

Borrowing Money

XII. The decisions of the courts with reference to various problems concerned with the borrowing of money are in a state of confusion.

A common method of placing debt burdens upon future generations is the careless use of the borrowing power. An adequate treatment of the statutory laws and legal decisions would constitute a sizable task in itself. Most of the states regulate in some way or another the borrowing power of the school districts. Cases are constantly before the courts upon this troublesome question which is a very convincing type of evidence that the matter has not been solved by our legislatures. In many states the statutes with reference to this matter cover many pages. The matter of borrowing for current expenses is usually subject to and sometimes part of the same constitutional or statutory limitation as that relating to the issuance of bonds for building purposes. This adds to the complexity of this phase of school administration. What constitutes the total indebtedness of a school district is a question which arises very frequently. Every change in statutory law regulating finances in any way means some change in matters relative to borrowing power, and so the problem grows. Halsey has made a study of this problem from the general economic point of view and includes a study of the legal control of the borrowing of money for the schools in the State of Florida.[111]

A few cases bearing directly upon the administrative phases of this problem of borrowing will be cited. In the case of Shonk Land Co. *v.* Joachim, *supra*, the board of education attempted to liquidate a floating debt of $84,190.18 by placing the amount as an item in its budget. The court would not permit this to be done. A similar decision was rendered in Oklahoma,[112] but a Kentucky Court of Appeals held such a procedure to be legal.[113] The general rule is that a debt in excess of the constitutional or statutory limitations is void,[114] but it has been held that only that portion in excess of the debt limit is void.[115]

Where a party has loaned money in good faith to a school district and it is used for lawful school purposes, the same can be recovered.[116] This rule was to hold even though the borrowing was void for irregularity. In this case, however, it was held incumbent upon the plaintiff to show that the money had been actually used for a lawful purpose.

A Florida court is somewhat conservative in the tenor of its decision for it permits a school district to pay debts out of current revenue, ". . . provided that the necessary expenses of maintaining the schools in any county during any year shall constitute a first claim against the school fund of that year." [117]

Quotations from other jurisdictions would only add to the confusion, since statutory provisions are different in each of the several states. It may be pointed out here that serious studies of this problem are needed. Before a really defensible code can be developed for this field, the law will have to await answers of a scientific nature to such problems as: How much indebtedness could and should a locality of any given wealth be allowed to carry? Should floating debts in the form of warrants be permitted? Should school districts create a surplus to be used as an operating fund so that no borrowing be necessary? Many other problems of a more detailed nature may be subject to more careful regulation than we at present dictate, such as rate of interest, time

[111] Halsey, H. R., *Borrowing Money for the Public Schools.*

[112] Gulf Pipe Line Co. *v.* County Treasurer, 110 Okla. 163, 236 P. 806 (1925).

[113] Elliot Co. Fiscal Court *v.* Elliot Co. Board of Education, Ky. 234 S. W. 947 (1921).

[114] Edwards *v.* School District No. 222, Cotton Co., 117 Okla. 269, 235 P. 611 (1925).

[115] Reisen *et al v.* School District No. 4, Village of Shorewood, 208 Wis. N. W. 762 (1926).

[116] First Nat. Bank Durand *v.* School District No. 1, Pepin, 187 Wis. 547,203 N. W. 762 (1925).

[117] Langford *v.* Odom, 77 Fla. 282, 81 So. 469 (1919).

of collection of taxes, and the payment of state aid grants to local school districts. Possible safeguards under which money may be borrowed from within the school organization itself need to be carefully studied. The pension funds now rapidly accumulating in several of the states and the sinking funds held for the payment of bonded indebtedness need to be surveyed and considered in this light.

DEFICITS

XIII. Neither the courts nor the legislatures have discovered any certain means of prohibiting deficits in expenditures for public schools.

In spite of numerous laws passed to keep schools as well as other spending bodies from creating deficits, the problem still remains unsolved. A study of the deficits of ninety-one Iowa cities [118] in 1921 showed that over one-half of the schools of the state were expending more than the legal limit of taxation. The Chicago schools were $12,000,000 in debt in December 1928.[119]

This problem is not new. In 1883 the Indiana legislature sought to clear up the indebtedness of her school districts which in some way had accumulated debts, contrary to a positive act of the Legislature.[120]

Oklahoma [121] schools "running behind" in funds have two methods of legally meeting such deficits. First, have warrants reduced to judgment and make a tax levy for the payment of the judgment. Second, issue funding bonds for the payment of the deficit.

A deficit in the form of outstanding indebtedness might be included in the next budget and paid,[122] but the same indebtedness shall not be included in the budget for two successive years.[123]

The statutes of the several states are very inadequate with reference to the handling of deficits. An examination of the statutes found very few of the states definitely recognizing the fact that there may be deficits and then meeting this question

[118] Lindsay, R. E., "A Study in School Deficits," *American School Board Journal*, 64: 47–48, February 1922.

[119] *New York Times*, December 28, 1928, p. 1.

[120] Jefferson School Township *v.* Litton, 116 Ind. 467, 19 N. E. 323.

[121] Gulf Pipe Line Co. *v.* County Treasurer, 108 Okla. 292, 236 P. 896 (1925).

[122] Elliott County Fiscal Court *v.* Elliott County Board of Education, Ky. 234 S. W. 947 (1921).

[123] County Board of Education, Daviess Co. *v.* Fiscal Court, 221 Ky. 111,298 S. W. 185 (1927).

squarely. Alabama directs, in a new code covering schools (1927), that the "city Council or Commission shall make such appropriation as will care for the deficit from the treasury of the city, if at all practicable to do so." One can imagine the city council making strenuous efforts to pay the deficits of the schools. The statutes of Georgia provide that actual deficits may be paid from funds which might have been originally appropriated for the purpose. This statute was upheld in the courts.[124] Idaho and Michigan direct that the deficit shall be taken care of in the levy of next year, while Massachusetts and Oregon have a reserve and contingent fund, respectively, to care for possible deficits. New Jersey provides that deficits may be voted in the same manner that the original budget was provided, and New York allows additional funds to be raised by means of a vote of the people. Mississippi provides for a deficit but another part of the law absolutely prohibits any deficit; while Utah says the people should vote bonds for the covering of deficits or certain types but does not say what is to happen if the bond issue should not carry. These are the only states which recognize the possibility of deficits and attempt to provide for them. There are, of course, provisions for emergencies in some states which are discussed elsewhere in this study. This investigator has found no authority advocating any other effective means of preventing deficits than those suggested in this code. Careful budgeting, holding authorities to the budget, good accounting, and control of the borrowing power are the most effective methods found.

Schools Closed for Lack of Funds

A Georgia [125] board, finding itself in debt $95,000, decided to close the schools for a time until such revenues as were levied would pay off the indebtedness. The court upheld its decision. The Washington Courts [126] also consider that the financing of the schools is more important than keeping them open. The court said:

> The maintenance of a public school throughout a school year of 8 months is not such a necessity as to warrant school directors in over-riding statutory and constitutional limitations as to the amount of indebtedness a school district may lawfully incur.

---

[124] Board of Education *v.* Thurmond, 162 Ga. 58, 132 S. E. 427 (1926). [125] *Ibid.*
[126] Wolfe *v.* School District No. 2, 58 Wash. 212, 108 P. 442 (1910).

It seems to be rather fundamental that the schools of a state must be kept open at all times. Certainly the children should not be penalized because of the carelessness or ignorance of those entrusted with their care. A code to care adequately for this possibility must be so constructed that the schools must continue in operation.[127]

SURPLUS FUNDS

XIV. In the absence of statutory provisions, there is no general rule as to the use to which a school board may put surplus funds.

The Educational Finance Inquiry [128] discovered the fact that in New York State there were numerous instances of the accumulation of surplus funds by many school districts. Certain cities had sums in excess of the yearly requirements which would have permitted those cities to finance their schools for an entire year without any local tax levy. The practice of accumulating large surpluses is a violation of the principle that the revenues of any given year shall pay the expenses of that year. The practice is condemned by Strayer and Haig in the study cited.

What have the courts said with reference to the accumulation and use of these surpluses? Texas [129] says that surplus funds may be used for any purpose for which the district might have originally provided these funds. In the fiscally dependent Massachusetts city of Cambridge,[130] the right of the board to keep control of the surplus funds ($37,818) with the purpose in view of taking care of the automatic increases in salary was upheld. Additional revenue from the gross production oil tax, coming unexpectedly after the budget adoption, was permitted to be used to aid in the erection of a new school building [131] upon the theory that the funds would not be diverted. The court held that it was none of the treasurer's or county commissioner's affair as to the probable disposition of such surplus funds.[132]

Missouri is not so liberal in her control of surplus funds but keeps them for the teacher's fund;[133] while California by statute re-

---

[127] Proposed Code, Art. VI, sec. 10.

[128] Strayer, George D. and Haig, R. M., *Educational Finance Inquiry*, Vol. I.

[129] Adams *v.* Miles, Texas 300 S. W. 211 (1927).

[130] Hunter *v.* Quinn, Mass. 138 N. E. 382 (1923).

[131] Board of Education *v.* Corey, Okla. 163 P. 949 (1917).

[132] School Commission Carter Co. *v.* School District No. 19, 119 Okla. 20, 248 P. 324.

[133] State *ex rel.* Holtz *v.* Bowman, Mo. 294 S. W. 107 (1927).

quires surplus funds of the county which are not used in the individual school districts to revert to the county and to be reapportioned as new moneys would be apportioned.[134] This is still the law in California, having been upheld in the case of Fawcett *v.* Ball, *supra*, decided in 1926. Waterbury, Connecticut, had a school board which did not expend $18,000 of an appropriation for a new school building, which the court directed to be returned to the city treasury.[135] This case has never been cited showing that cases of this nature seldom arise.

> It is therefore necessary to inquire which is preferable in public financiering: close estimates with probable deficits and temporary loans to cover them, or loose estimates with broad margins for contingencies, with a probable surplus. . . . We answer without hesitation that a wise fiscal policy will approve deficit rather than surplus financiering.[136]

This conclusion of Adams's is agreed to by authorities and is used as the basis for the placing of the hurdles in this suggested code.[137] It is definitely planned to discourage the piling up of large surpluses during any fiscal period.

---

[134] Kennedy *v.* Miller Co. Treas., 97 Cal. 429. 32 P. 558 (1893).
[135] Chatfield Co. *v.* City of Waterbury, 88 Conn. 322, 91 A. 436 (1914).
[136] Adams, H. C., *The Science of Finance*, p. 528.
[137] Proposed Code, Art. VI, sec. 14.

CHAPTER VI

THE CITY GOVERNMENT AND ITS CONTROL OVER SCHOOL EXPENDITURES

The legal principles to be discussed in this chapter are:

I. The courts have generally upheld the power of the board of education to control the purposes for which school funds may be expended, even in fiscally dependent cities.

II. A school board is not subject to regulation by provisions in either a special or home-rule charter, when the same are in conflict with the general laws of the state controlling schools. Should the legislature desire to allow the city government power of control over school finances, it must definitely delegate such authority by general or special act.

III. ". . . From the very dawn of our liberties, the principle most unquestionable of all has been this: that the people shall vote the taxes they are to pay, or be permitted to choose representatives for that purpose." [1]

IV. The school system of a state is a matter of general concern as distinguished from a "municipal affair."

Educational literature has on record several studies and numerous discussions upon the relative fiscal rights of the city government and the board of education. The control of expenditures as exercised by control over income is of extreme importance and has been conducive to much serious thinking on the part of educational administrators. The evidence given here will present decisions defining certain phases of this control.

Fiscal Control of School Expenditures by the City Government

Conflict Recognized by the Courts

I. The courts have generally upheld the power of the board of education to control the purposes for which school funds may be expended, even in fiscally dependent cities.

[1] Judge Cooley in opinion rendered in case of People *ex rel.* Park Commissioners *v.* Common Council, Detroit, 28 Mich. 228, 15 A. M. Rep. 202 (1873).

The courts have recognized this conflict, and a very comprehensive statement was made of the problem by Judge Davis of the Buffalo Division of the New York Appellate Court in 1922:

It has already been recognized that the provisions of law governing the duties of boards of education and of municipal authorities are somewhat in conflict. It is difficult to see how it could be otherwise, when a separate corporate body is created as a department of the city and is entitled to demand and receive funds from moneys raised by taxation in the city, yet claiming the right to act independently of the legislative and administrative departments of government of the city. The municipal authorities would naturally seek to apply to this department of the city government those provisions of law contained in its charter and elsewhere applicable to other departments. No doubt with this conflict in mind, if the municipal officers and the members of the board of education realized that they were engaged in a common purpose, to wit, to expend moneys received from taxation in the most economical and efficient manner possible for the public welfare, they could meet in a spirit of conciliation and agree upon some policy that would accomplish the desired result without straining to assert and maintain abstract rights and prerogatives. In the experiences we have thus far had, no such spirit has been manifest.[2]

Power of the City to Dictate Expenditure Program

In the case of Reif *v.* Schwab, *supra*, Judge Davis held that the city council:

. . . may in its discretion reduce the amount demanded by the estimate; but the reduction must be in gross amount. The detailed items are, I think, to give the council information and aid in determining the total amount to be appropriated. The reduction in items of salaries or expenditures made by the council are, I think of no more effect than the suggestion that in its judgment such reductions are advisable. Its action may point out to the board the reasons for making the reduction from the total estimate and indicate the items least necessary for the proper and economical management of the schools. I think such changes are advisory only; and, while entitled to great consideration as coming from the body in general control of the city government and particularly of its finances and taxation, are not controlling.

Another Buffalo case in the Erie County Supreme Court (1927) upheld the right of the board of education of the city of Buffalo to select and purchase a site for a school building.[3] As long as the board acted in the manner prescribed by law, the city of Buffalo, through its city council, had to pay the bill and had to raise the funds to pay for it even though the funds were not available at that particular time.

[2] Rief *v.* Schwab, 204 N. Y. App. 50.

[3] Kane Cadillac Co. *v.* City of Buffalo, 128 Misc. Rep. 835, 221 N. Y. S. 167.

The case of Fleishmann *v.* Graves[4] was taken to the New York Court of Appeals in 1923, and the Court held that the city council under the Educational Law of New York State had power to determine whether or not expenditures are legal.

> The duty of the city officials under the Education Law and the charter of the city of Buffalo is: First, to appropriate money for educational purposes according to the proposed estimates readjusted by the city council in making up its budget for all departments of the city, so as to keep within the constitutional tax limitation. Second, to see that the moneys so raised and placed to the credit of the educational fund shall not be used for purposes other than those authorized by the Education Law. With the particular items going to make up the estimate, which includes salaries for teachers, employees, servants, and other persons assisting in the administration of educational affairs, the city has no particular concern except that it may direct how funds are classified.

Such power given to the city auditor or comptroller to determine what constitutes an educational expenditure under the educational laws seems conducive to much legal conflict in New York State. This practice is essentially wrong in principle. Since the schools are state institutions, it seems that their expenditures should not be subject to practically judicial supervision by a city ministerial officer. The numerous cases concerning the administration of expenditures arising in this jurisdiction are evidence that such authority is wrongly placed.

The New Jersey courts uphold the doctrine that the city council after making an appropriation has no power to dictate the distribution and disbursement of money, even though the budget was itemized and the appropriations were specific.[5]

The city council of Binghamton, New York, sought, in 1915, to investigate the affairs of the board of education under the general power given in the city charter to "regulate the powers and duties of any department and investigate all city officers and departments." The principle involved in this case was held by the court to be that the city has no power to investigate or supervise the affairs of the board of education where it could not give constructive aid.

> . . . It is a strong presumption that the power given to a municipality to investigate is ancillary only to the power to regulate. It is not probable that the common council has been given power to uncover a sore that it cannot heal. . . . To the extent to which the common council is authorized to

[4] Fleishmann *v.* Graves, 235 N. Y. S. 84, 138 N. E. 745 (1923).

[5] Townsend *v.* State Board of Education, 88 N. J. L. 97, 95 A. 729 (1915).

regulate the powers and duties of the board of education, it is clearly authorized to investigate and it will naturally follow that the limit of the power to regulate would be the limit of the power to investigate. . . . Moreover, there are economic reasons which imperatively demand a complete separation between the educational and political departments of a city, as far as the regulation of the public schools is concerned. If the members of a board of education were subject at all times to examination and investigation by a political municipal body, it would seriously impair the usefulness of the board and materially interfere with the highest efficiency.[6]

The power of the city government to regulate expenditures has received several setbacks in New York City. In a recent case the Board of Estimate and Apportionment was not allowed any directive power over the funds once they were appropriated to the board of education.[7]

The board of estimate and apportionment cannot supersede the Education Law by tacking on to its appropriations for school purposes limitations upon the power of the board of education given it by the Education Law. The board of estimate may grant or refuse the appropriations, but once having made them, the Education Law enacts how they shall be used.

This Brennan case upheld the principles enunciated in the leading case in this field of law, that of Gunnison *v.* Board of Education:

The city cannot rent, build, or buy a schoolhouse. It cannot employ or discharge a teacher, and has no power to contract with teachers with reference to their compensation. There is no contract or official relation, express or implied, between the teachers and the city. All this results from the settled policy of the state from an early date to divorce the business of public education from all other municipal interests or business and to take charge of it as its peculiar and separate function, through agents of its own selection, and immediately subject and responsive to its own control. . . . The only relation the city has to the subject of public education is as custodian and depositary of school funds, and its only duty with respect to that fund is to keep it safely and disburse the same according to the instructions of the board of education. The city, as trustee, has title to the money, but it is under the care, control, and administration of the boards of education.[8]

One of the clearest and most forceful opinions upon this matter of fiscal control was enunciated in Michigan in 1925. This opinion points out the ultimate outcome of control of school finances by a city fiscal body and an understanding of the infor-

[6] Miller *v.* Tayntor, 170 N. Y. App. 126, 155 N. Y. S. 746 (1915).
[7] Brennan *v.* Board of Education, 245 N. Y. S. 8, 156 N. E. 78 (1927).
[8] Gunnison *v.* Board of Education, 176 N. Y. 11, 68 N. E. 106 (1903).

mation which is necessary to the formulation of a defensible program of financial policy. The court said:

If the defendant is right, then the legislature must have intended, in effect, to take from the school board and give to the board of estimate the power to determine, from which no right of appeal or review is given, the length of the school year under the statute, the number and compensation of teachers, the fiscal plans and policies, and the character and quality of materials, supplies, and equipment of the school district; for, if the board of estimate has power to say upon the estimate how much and for what purpose money may be raised, it is, by its absolute power of veto, virtually the master of the plaintiff district.

This was not intended. If it were, we might expect to find a clear legislative expression to that effect. The statute makes no provision for supplying the board of estimates with facts, data, statistics, reports, etc., so that an intelligent judgment on the matter might be passed, nor does it require the school board to exhibit its affairs, its needs, its problems to the board of estimates. It was the intent of the Constitution to separate the school organization from the general municipal government, and to turn the whole subject over to the legislature. . . .

So long as the board of education stayed within the tax limit and within the law, as it did, it was answerable to no one, except the electors of the district.[9]

The above decision sounds almost as if a school administrator had written it.

City Government and Control of Salaries of School Employees

The statutes in many states and the great weight of legal opinion places the control of salaries of employees of schools in the board of education. Many states are reserving as a state right the power to exercise certain controls over salaries paid to teachers.

Even in fiscally dependent cities, the courts have been emphatic in maintaining that the city shall not control the salaries of the teachers. One of the leading cases comes from Massachusetts, still one of the bulwarks in maintaining the dependence of school authorities upon the city for its finances.[10] In this case the budget as submitted by the board of education carried an increase in salaries for teachers. The mayor refused to approve the budget and submitted a reduced budget to the council. The city council dodged the issue by failing to take action within the time provided by statute, and the reduced budget was *ipso facto* adopted. However, the board then finding itself with a reduced income planned

[9] Board of Education, Saginaw, East Side *v.* Board of Estimates, 230 Mich. 495, 203 N. W. 68 (1925).

[10] Leonard *v.* School Committee, Mass., 135 N. E. 459 (1922).

certain changes in the estimate. It wished to pay the teachers the increases, and in order to get the money to do this it eliminated summer schools and kindergartens, and curtailed certain other expenses. The question came up to the court as to whether or not this change in the budget as made by the school committee was legal. The court held:

> The school committee is an independent body, entrusted by the law with certain broad powers, important duties, and large discretion. The obligation to select and contract with teachers implies examination as to their fitness and of necessity carries with it the power to fix the compensation to be paid. It would be vain to impose upon the school committee responsibility for excellence of instruction to be afforded to pupils and to deprive them of the power to determine the salaries of teachers. There is much of self-sacrifice and devotion to the common welfare among teachers in the public schools. But, nevertheless, the character of service to be obtained depends to a considerable degree upon the compensation offered. The full and appropriate discharge of their duties by school committees requires ample power to select competent teachers. . . . In the exercise of their honest judgment on the question of salaries for teachers the school committee are not restricted to the amounts appropriated. . . . The only supervision which the city council or towns can exercise over the school committee is to vote to close the schools after they have been kept open the time specified by the law.

This decision was upheld in 1925 and strengthened when the court[11] dictated that the city council must provide salaries as estimated in the budget voted by the school committee.

In the State of New York, the city governments have in recent years been having trouble in retaining power over teachers' and supervisors' salaries. The case of Fuhrmann *v.* Graves[12] in Buffalo (1923) had as its principal issue the proper residuum of the power to fix the salary of the superintendent of schools. The city council attempted to limit the power of the board by refusing to grant the appropriation to the amount asked by the board for that purpose. Judge McLaughlin said:

> The intent of the legislature in enacting the Education Law is clear. It imposes on boards of education as separate corporate bodies, representing the state, the responsibility of furnishing an efficient system of public education and in this respect are not subject to or controlled by the city authorities. . . . As to when, how, and where the amounts placed at their disposal shall be disbursed, each board exercises an independent judgment uncontrolled by and in no respect influenced by city authorities.

[11] Decatur *et al.* *v.* Peabody, 251 Mass. 82, 146 N. E. 360 (1925).

[12] Fuhrmann *v.* Graves, 235 N. Y. 77, 138 N. E. 743.

The same principle was upheld recently in Michigan.

> If the board of estimate may cut the salary of the Superintendent of Schools $500, as it did in the instant case, it may cut it in halves and prevent the hiring of a competent man because of the inadequacy of the salary. This also applies to other items which were reduced.[13]

However, by express charter provision,[14] the Board of Aldermen in New York City fix the salaries of janitors in public schools,[15] of copyists in the office of the board of education,[16] and of all other employees of the board of education except day laborers, teachers, and members of the supervisory staff.[17]

Control by City Over Other Expenditures

A New England town may not require that money raised by it shall be applied to any special purpose.[18] The appropriation of school money rests exclusively with the school board.[19] Vermont, in the case of Farmer *v.* Haley (1926), rules that the right to purchase supplies rests with the board of education, but that the repairing of school buildings shall be done by the town manager and paid for by the board of education.[20] This case also held that the right to employ janitors was a power of the board of education.

A city ordinance which fixes a minimum wage scale of 75 cents per hour for laborers working upon all public works does not apply to the erection of schoolhouses, even though contracts for school buildings run in the name of the city and are countersigned by the mayor and approved by the city attorney.[21] The above case also gave the board the exclusive power to select sites and erect school buildings.

The principle seems fairly well established in New York, New Jersey, and Massachusetts that the control of expenditures of school districts by the city government is limited to a control of the total amount to be expended and does not extend to control of the purposes for which money is to be expended. As

[13] Union School District *v.* Council, City of Saginaw, 232 Mich. 639, 206 N. W. 573 (1925).
[14] Charter, Greater New York, Ash., p. 68, sec. 56 and ch. I, as amended January, 1925.
[15] Mahoney *v.* Board of Education, New York, 167 N. Y. S. 222, 179 App. Div. 782 (1917).
[16] Dobrovolney *v.* Prendergast, 219 N. Y. 280, 114 N. E. 436 (1916).
[17] Hogan *v.* City of New York, 137 App. Div. 255 (1910).
[18] Wheeler *v.* City of Alton, 68 N. H. 477, 38 A. 208 (1896).
[19] Bailey *v.* Duffy, R. I. 121 A. 129 (1923).
[20] Farmer *v.* Haley, Vt. 135 A. 12.
[21] Schmidt and Son, Inc. *v.* Milwaukee, 185 Wis. 119, 200 N. W. 678 (1924).

these states are among the principal bulwarks of city control over school fiscal powers, this limitation of the city's power is important.

The City Charter and Its Power to Control Expenditures

II. A school board is not subject to regulation by provisions in either a special or home-rule charter, when the same are in conflict with the general laws of the state controlling schools. Should the legislature desire to allow the city government power of control over school finances, it must definitely delegate such authority by general or special act.

The general state laws relating to educational organization and procedure have been held superior to both special and home-rule charters. This principle was upheld in the case of Brennan *v.* Board of Education, and also in the case of Fuhrmann *v.* Graves, both of which cases have been cited herein.

The San Francisco Board of Education is not subject to charter regulations by the city but to the state statutes, at least in those matters where the state speaks or has not definitely given the city power to regulate. Such regulations even then must not be in conflict with the general state laws.[22]

The city of Port Huron, Michigan, sought, under a statute permitting the city to adopt its own charter, to establish and enforce a charter provision whereby the city council should have complete authority over the finances of the schools. The court held that the city could not exercise any such power.[23] The above case was upheld in principle again in Michigan (1925) in the case of Union School District *v.* Council, City Saginaw, *supra.*

The Tax Levy

III. "From the very dawn of our liberties, the principle most unquestionable of all has been this: that the people shall vote the taxes they are to pay, or be permitted to choose representatives for that purpose."—Judge Cooley.[24]

The control of the amount of taxes to be raised has been one of the most thoroughly discussed problems in school administration. Such control is a most powerful regulator of control over

[22] Esberg *v.* Badaracco, 202 Cal. 110, 259 P. 730 (1927).

[23] McQueen *v.* City Commission, Port Huron, 194 Mich. 328, 160 N. W. 627 (1916).

[24] People *ex rel.* Park Commissioners *v.* Common Council of Detroit, 28 Mich. 228, 15 AM. Rep. 202 (1873).

expenditures. Without money to expend, the school board may be unable to put into effect educational policies which it may deem fundamental.

This study of the law has enabled this investigator to focus more light upon a most important additional argument for the fiscal independence of school boards. The evidence is presented in as brief form as is consistent with its importance as a principle of democratic control.

> Perhaps no principle is more characteristic of our political system than the doctrine that there shall be no taxation without representation.[25]
>
> Accordingly, after the American Revolution, the states uniformly adopted constitutions which vested the taxing power primarily in legislative bodies.[26]
>
> As already observed, the right of taxation is vested in the people; but legislation is necessary to exercise the right of taxation. Under our form of government, this legislative power is vested (in the first instance) in the legislature of the State. The Legislature, in the exercise of its sovereign power, may confer upon minor subdivisions of the State power to impose and levy local rates . . . on the principle that for local purposes the local authorities are representatives of the people.[27]

How carefully the courts guard this right is shown in this last case where the court refused to allow an appointed commission of three resident freeholders (even though the statute so directed the governor to appoint such a commission) to assess and levy taxes when the regular taxing authority neglected or refused to act. The principle involved was that the tax-levying power could not be delegated to any except duly elected representatives of the people. This case gives an excellent history of the fight for popular control over taxation and cites the controversy which existed in New Jersey Colonial Assembly 1748–1752. In this period the "Council" sought to amend an appropriation bill of the "Assembly" to which the latter body would not agree, holding that the power to appropriate money belonged to them. The controversy lasting four years left the colonial government for this period without funds to pay its bills. Our early forefathers did not compromise on principles.

The principle that the power to tax cannot be delegated to appointed boards was enunciated in North Dakota in 1907:

---

[25] Thomas *v.* Gay, 169 U. S. 264 (1898).

[26] Gray, J. M., *Limitations on the Taxing Power*, pp. 583–615.

[27] Inhabitants Town of Bernard *v.* Allen *et al.*, 61 N. J. L. 228, 38 A. 716 (1898).

> The power of the legislature to delegate the authority to levy taxes is generally held to be limited to boards or councils elected by the people, and it is not sanctioned when delegated to those appointed, when the appointment has not been assented to by a vote of the people. This limitation is recognized under the general principle that all powers of taxation are reposed in the people, and unless the people assent by vote to the appointment or election of the taxing authorities such powers of taxation not thus assented to are repugnant to the Constitution and not to be upheld. The power to levy taxes is one of the most important legislative functions. If abused, it may amount to a practical confiscation of property. . . . A power so far-reaching should not be reposed in any one not directly responsible to the people. If appointed by the people and abuses follow, a remedy by removal is in their hands; otherwise, redress is so remote as to be without practical results.[28]

This case has been cited many times and has been upheld as late as 1928.[29]

The following decision is not law;[30] it was gotten from the dissenting opinion of three of the seven judges of the Pennsylvania Supreme Court, but this opinion is regarded [31] as sounder law in principle than that of the majority of the court. It is cited much more often.

Judge Brown wrote this dissenting opinion concerning the power and right of an appointed board of education to levy taxes:

> These directors are not true representatives of the people. . . . The scheme is one of bald taxation without representation and strikes at the very root of a republican form of government, for taxes are a grant of the people and the grant must be by their immediate representatives. The people are not to be taxed except by their own consent or that of officers truly representing them.

Thus it is seen that the legal authorities, in what is regarded as sound law and political theory, state in no uncertain terms the principle of popular control over finances. The law will not generally uphold the right of appointed boards to levy taxes, maintaining that the people must have direct control over the officials who have the right to make a demand upon the public purse. Why, then, should the people release this power of control to a third party? It is maintained that the delegation of the power of making a tax levy or the approval of a tax levy to a city council or other fiscal body removes control farther from the people. Certainly, control is more direct and positive when

[28] Vallelly *et al.* *v.* Board of Park Commissioners, 16 N. D. 25, 111 N. W. 615 (1907).

[29] State *v.* Curtis, Mo. 4 S. W. 2nd 467.

[30] Minsinger *v.* Rau, Pa. 84 A. 902 (1912).

[31] *Harvard Law Review*, 26: 257.

exercised over a board of education, the sole duty of which is to administer the school policies and finances, than it would be over any other body charged with multifarious duties and responsibilities. Just how would the citizens of New York City or any other fiscally dependent city go about the proposition of definitely expressing their disapproval of the policies and financial management of their city schools? Why should the people delegate authority to a fiscal body with but incidental power of redress when they may exercise direct control themselves upon definite issues?

Another argument for fiscal independence of school boards has not been urged to the extent which it seems to merit. Fiscal dependence tends to make the school district coterminous with the city boundary and thus deters and almost prevents an organization of school districts on bases other than those of present political subdivisions of governmental units. In this day when the slogan for equality of opportunity is leading us into new fields of thought, the location of the homes of pupils, transportation facilities, financial resources, ease and efficiency of administration and other justifiable criteria should determine the size and nature of a school district rather than simply political boundaries. The growth of the county unit organization in the several states is evidence of the soundness of this argument. One of the latest surveys made by Strayer and Engelhardt advocates for Chattanooga, Tennessee, and Hamilton County, a school district embracing the entire county as well as the city. Their principal arguments are those mentioned above, namely, that such an organization, in view of such factors as those mentioned, will furnish to the children of that community the nearest possible approach to equality of opportunity.[32]

Schools Are Not Municipal Affairs

IV. The school system of a state is a matter of general concern as distinguished from a "municipal affair."

Certain of the critics in the field of municipal administration are making much of the argument that the city as well as the school district is an instrumentality of the state. Let a California Court make an added distinction.

---

[32] *Report of the Survey of Certain Aspects of the School System of Chattanooga and Hamilton County, Tennessee.* Strayer, G. D., and Engelhardt, N. L., Directors.

> But with the school department we are confronted by different and controlling considerations of the law. The school system of the state is a matter of general concern as distinguished from a "municipal affair," as that term is considered in connection with charter cities. . . . By this article of the Constitution, the people of the state have made the school system a matter of state supervision, and judicial declarations to the same effect are numerous.[33]

There is a difference between the relationship of the school district to the state and that of a city to the state. Have we a state system of cities? Is it the concern of the state that every city have an electric light plant? A trolley or bus system? Paved streets or sidewalks? It is true, however, that every state does have a state system of schools. It is the concern of the state that every school building be erected according to certain standards which insure the health and safety of the children. It is the business of the state that the children be taught by teachers having certain qualifications and that these teachers receive a wage in keeping with the responsibility and standard of living which they should set for the community. It is the business of the state that every teacher and every child shall have suitable materials with which to work. The state is concerned with many other items which might be mentioned as being necessary for the development of the school program. Until the city administrators and the critics who advocate the fiscal dependence of the schools upon the city can point to more efficient returns per dollar of tax money expended than can the schools in analogous situations, their arguments will not greatly concern the school administrators.

Research by at least two students of educational administration has presented strong evidence that the control of the amount of income should rest with the board of education. Frasier made a careful study in which he proved, by the application of certain defensible criteria, that fiscal independence works better in practice.[34] McGaughy proved that the schools in fiscally independent cities did not cost more than those in fiscally dependent cities, which fact took away the most important argument the "fiscally dependent" theorists had. McGaughy [35] also presented evidence of other types to substantiate Frasier's study.

[33] Esberg *v.* Badaracco, 202 Cal. 110, 259 P. 730 (1927).

[34] Frasier, G. W., *The Control of City School Finance*, pp. 83–87.

[35] McGaughy, J. R., *The Fiscal Administration of City School Systems*, The Educational Finance Inquiry, Vol. V.

The leading proponent for school authorities has been George D. Strayer. He has studied this problem for a quarter of a century. During recent years he has been ably assisted by N. L. Engelhardt, and most of the studies in this field have had their encouragement, aid, advice and direction.

Many other authorities might be cited as favoring fiscal dependence. It is not the primary purpose of this study to review the excellent arguments and proof presented by those who have studied this field more intensively. The law relating to control of expenditures through control of income had to be studied and the contribution of the law to their field was brought to light.

The advocates of the fiscal dependence of the school authorities upon the city government come from the authorities upon municipal administration.[36]

In the proposed code the tax levying power is given to the board of education.[37] The evidence both from the law and the research as to its practical application warrants an unequivocal statute on the matter.

---

[36] Anderson, Wm., *American City Government*, pp. 90–96; Buck, A. E., *Municipal Finance*, pp. 27–30; Goodnow, F. J., *Municipal Government*, Chap. XVI.

[37] See Proposed Code, Art. VII, sec. 1.

CHAPTER VII

LEGAL CONTROL OVER THE ADMINISTRATION OF CONTRACTS

Provisions for the Purpose of Securing Honesty, Economy, and Efficiency of Administration

The law as it relates to contracts is most complex. There are many types of control over the administration of school expenditures which come from the general law of contracts. This study has taken a few phases of legal control which the courts have had trouble in solving and which are important to the effective administration of school expenditures.

The following principles will be discussed in this chapter:

I. In order to delegate the power to execute the expenditure program to the superintendent of schools or to the business manager, the legislature must either definitely grant such power to such officer or direct in specific terms that the board of education may delegate such authority.

II. When a statute requires certain formalities of a board of education in the execution of a contract involving the expenditure of funds, restrictions as to the form and manner of action will be rigidly enforced.

III. The general rule is that contracts will not be implied as against a school board.

IV. When a contract has been made by a board of education and it is afterwards found that it is unauthorized, the courts have not formulated any set rules concerning the right of the board to ratify the contract. It is generally upheld that an illegal contract cannot be ratified.

V. Statutes requiring that contracts under certain restrictions must be awarded only after notice and a call for proposals or bids will be strictly enforced. An important exception is that contracts for personal service are usually not held to be within the requirement.

VI. When a statute directs that the contract "shall be awarded to the lowest bidder," the courts are inclined to interpret the statute rather strictly. However, if the language is less mandatory, the courts will usually allow the board some discretion in awarding the contract.

VII. The courts interpret strictly those statutes which prohibit personal financial interest of board members or school officials in contracts made for the school district. The common law, in the absence of statute, prohibits such an interest.

Delegation of Power to Make Expenditures

I. In order to delegate the power to execute the expenditure program to the superintendent of schools or to the business manager, the legislature must either definitely grant such power to such officer or direct in specific terms that the board of education may delegate such authority.

An examination of the statutes (1927) shows that in comparatively few states has any provision been made to delegate the expenditure program to the superintendent of schools or to a business manager.[1]

Authorities are ardently supporting the theory that the board of education's principal function is the legislative one and that the executive powers be transferred to its professional officers. It is interesting and surprising to notice the lack of statutory authorization and definite delegation of this power to these officers. The legislature must definitely confer this power upon the professional officers or it must give the school board power to so delegate this authority to execute the expenditure program.

An examination of the cases on this subject shows the necessity for this type of a statute. A leading case from Illinois is cited.[2]

---

[1] The superintendent of schools may be delegated with the power to make expenditures in Connecticut and in certain districts in Maine.

Kentucky and New Jersey provide for business managers in certain districts and give them limited power to make expenditures.

Illinois provides for a business manager for the city of Chicago and gives him power to make purchases under certain regulations.

Pennsylvania places the secretary in full charge of business affairs.

Ohio puts the "director" (business manager) in full charge.

The secretary or clerk of the board may be delegated authority to execute the board's wishes in California, Nevada, and Washington.

Utah says that authority may be delegated but does not say definitely to whom such powers may be given.

Tennessee delegates authority to the county superintendent and the chairman of the board.

Mississippi permits the county superintendent to contract with teachers.

Georgia delegates by statute executive authority to the county superintendent.

Indiana designates that expenditures be made by the district trustee, except in cities over 100,000 which may elect a business manager.

Washington makes the employment of a business manager optional.

The remainder of the states either have no provision for the delegation of the expenditure power, or the statutes are so indefinite as to be incapable of classification.

[2] National Bank of Decatur *v.* Board of Education, 205 Ill. App. 57 (1918).

In considering the sufficiency of these counts it must be kept in mind that the appellee is a municipal corporation and that as a general proposition it speaks only through its records and properly executed documents and that no person, committee, or officer of such a corporation can bind it by contract, unless he or they are expressly authorized to do so, or the power to do so is necessarily implied from the powers expressly given, and that such authority must be given by statute or by the corporation, acting within its powers in the manner provided by law. It must also be remembered that when authority to make a contract is given by such a corporation, that fact can only be shown by the record, and the contract when made under such authority must be ratified by a majority vote of the controlling board of such corporation, which vote can only be shown by the record of the corporation. We know of no exception to that general rule, where the contract is one of the character of the one before us.

The decision quoted above shows that school districts in Illinois are municipal corporations. As stated,[3] these corporations are the highest type of public corporations, and, therefore, the powers granted in other states where districts are only quasi-corporations would be even more strictly construed.

The Kentucky Court of Appeals is even more emphatic and points out that—

. . . in making the expense which it is allowed to make, the board should not delegate this power, either directly or indirectly, to another, not even to the superintendent.[4]

This principle was upheld in Kentucky in 1923,[5] Judge Sampson writing the opinion.

A municipal board like the appellant cannot confer by resolution, order or otherwise, its powers involving the exercise of discretion. The resolution authorizing Davenport to "build another room and add a porch to the schoolhouse" was invalid because it undertook to vest him with the power to exercise the discretion reposed in the board.

An equally important decision was rendered in Connecticut and the syllabus of the case states briefly the court's decision:[6]

. . . Chairman of committee in informing plaintiff of award of contract held to act as messenger and not as agent. . . . Public officers or agents are held more strictly within their prescribed powers than a private or general agent and a contract made with a public agent within the apparent scope of his powers does not in the absence of estoppel or actual authority bind the principal.

---

[3] *Ante*, p. 14. [4] Beauchamp *v.* Snider, 170 Ky. 220, 185 S. W. 868 (1916).

[5] County Board of Education *v.* Durham, Ky., 239 S. W. 1028.

[6] Lucien *v.* Town of Norfolk, 99 Conn. 639, 122 A. 711 (1923).

The principle of not allowing any delegation of authority to contract involving the expenditure of money has been upheld in Indiana,[7] Tennessee,[8] and Wisconsin.[9]

The board of education may by definite action authorize an officer to do some act relating to expenditures of a purely ministerial nature.[10]

> The authorization to its secretary to accept an offer binding on the board of education was not an unlawful delegation of its powers. The price had been fixed, and the exercise of the power involved neither judgment nor discretion. The secretary's action was purely ministerial and perfunctory.

In Mississippi where such statutory authority is given to a county superintendent to contract with teachers, the power of the superintendent to pay teachers more than their contracts called for was upheld. This case seems basic in a broad interpretation of the superintendent's powers, but does not seem to have elicited much enthusiasm in other jurisdictions as it has been cited but a very few times since its rendition in 1916.[11]

> The superintendent is vested with both executive and judicial powers, and the efficiency of the public school system requires that large administrative powers be vested in him. In view of the fact, therefore, that the work paid for by the superintendent, and the several alleged irregularities were within the jurisdiction of his office and no corruption is charged, the bill fails to state a cause of action.

A decided contrast to the above broad interpretation of the superintendent's powers comes from California, a state which is generally agreed to be in the vanguard of progressive school systems but which evidently would not agree to vest the superintendent with any power of expenditure.[12]

> We have found nothing in the statutes, nor in the municipal charters, nor in the decisions of the higher courts of this state that defined the official status of a city superintendent. . . . His duties are apparently entirely ministerial and not outlined or enumerated by any law.

An Alabama case represents an illustration of the rather dubious grounds on which the contracts made by executive officers of the board rest.[13]

---

[7] Railroad School Township *v.* First State Bank, 73 Ind. A. 358, 126 N. E. 342 (1920).

[8] State *ex rel.* Milligan *v.* Jones, Tenn. 224, S. W. 104 (1920).

[9] School District Town Segal *v.* Industrial Commission, 194 Wis. 342, 216 N. W. 844 (1927).

[10] Ames *v.* Board of Education Montclair, N. J. 127, A. 95 (1925).

[11] State *v.* Green County Superintendent, 111 Miss. 32, 71 So. 171.

[12] Stewart *v.* Eaves, 84 Cal. A. 201, 257 P. 917 (1927).

[13] Greeson Manufacturing Co. *v.* County Board of Education, Ala. 117 So. 163 (1928).

The material was furnished and accepted, and used, however, for legitimate purposes entirely within the scope of the county boards' authority, and it therefore becomes its duty to reimburse the plaintiff therefor, not by virtue of the contract, but from the general obligation to do justice which binds all persons, natural and artificial.

The practice of delegating expenditures, however, is quite common. Ganders [14] reports that 85% of the 800 cities reporting recognize the superintendent as the leader in business affairs and that in 69% of these cities the superintendent authorizes the purchase orders.

Heer [15] reports that most of the business managers whose work he studied (29 out of 30 in one group, and 25 out of 26 in a second group) do the actual purchasing for the board of education and in many instances without approval by either the board or the superintendent.

Authorities in the field of education seem to be agreed that authority to execute the expenditure program should be delegated to the superintendent and in larger cities through him to the business manager.[16] Authorities in governmental finance also agree that the execution of the budget shall be an executive function.[17] The budget of the United States has always been under executive direction.

In the code proposed, Article VIII, section 3, provides for the delegation of the power to execute the expenditure program of the board of education to the superintendent of schools and through him to the business manager. It should be pointed out that this proposed code delegating power to the superintendent or other officer may not be upheld by the courts of some states. One reason for this statement is the strictness with which the courts have held the boards to formalities of action. A second reason is the hesitancy of the courts to allow the board of education to delegate its discretionary authority. It is believed, however, that the code provision will stand the test in most of the states.

---

[14] Ganders, H. W., *Personnel and Organization in Small Cities.* U. S. Bureau of Education, Bulletin No. 6, 1926, p. 5.

[15] Heer, A. L., *The Present Status of Business Executives in the Public Schools of the United States in Cities of 25,000 and More Inhabitants*, p. 104.

[16] Engelhardt, N. L. and Engelhardt, Fred, *Public School Business Administration*, p. 680; Heer, A. L., *op. cit.*, p. 131; Taylor, R. B., *Principles of School Supply Management*, pp. 12–13; Smith, H. P., *The Business Administration of a City School System*, p. 93.

[17] Stourm, René, *The Budget*, p. 53.

Administration of Contracts

Formalities Required

II. When a statute requires certain formalities of a board of education in the execution of a contract involving an expenditure of funds, restrictions as to the form and manner of action will usually be rigidly enforced.

A school board cannot bind itself or the school district, except when regularly convened and acting as an official body. The exercise of the right to expend money has been declared unlawful, in most jurisdictions, if done in any other manner. The general rule is stated in a recent Iowa decision.

> The doctrine is well established in this state, that individual directors of school districts cannot bind their districts by acts not authorized by the board, and we have held, that an act of a majority of such directors, when not assembled and acting as a board, will not bind the district.[18]

The courts are very strict in interpreting this rule, as is shown by an Illinois case where an informal conference of all the members of the board was held not to be a legal meeting. At this conference, the architect, all members of the board, and the contractor, met to discuss a way out of a building difficulty. The contractor due to a rapid rise of prices of labor and material was going into debt and losing money on the contract. The board members agreed informally that the contractor should go ahead with the work, keep an exact statement of the extra cost, and that the board would pay him the loss sustained. Board members testified that this was the general understanding of all present, but that the meeting was never formally called to order and that no resolution was adopted. The court held:

> Informal and uncertain action of this kind by various members of the board of education cannot be the basis of official action, under which the school district is to be burdened with an indebtedness of $24,500, and in the opinion of this court the district, by such action, never assumed any legal liability.
>
> Paragraph 119, Chapter 122, Cahill's Statutes, reads, "No official business shall be transacted by the directors except at a regular or special meeting." Paragraph 120 reads, "On all questions involving the expenditure of money, the yeas and nays shall be taken and entered on the records of the proceedings of the board."[19]

---

[18] Andrew *v.* Stuart Savings Bank, Iowa, 215 N. W. 803 (1927).

[19] Board of Education *v.* Barracks, 235 Ill. App. 35 (1924).

Other cases and authorities upholding this principle of no legal action except at a formal meeting may be cited.[20] However, it has been held that the place of meeting is not important, as a meeting has been held valid when held outside the school district.[21]

Kansas was the only jurisdiction in which a case was discovered which upholds the right of the board to act as individuals and thus bind the board in making an expenditure.[22]

Written Contracts

The common law rule was that all contracts with municipalities and other governmental units, in order to be valid, had to be in writing. The courts have not been any too consistent in their decisions made in cases involving statutes which require the formality of a written contract. The cases cited, *infra*, will illustrate the fact that statutes in derogation of the common law must be very carefully and concisely written, for such statutes will be strictly interpreted. A consideration of a case in the Wisconsin courts will show how courts will sometimes wander when new statutes in derogation of the common law are adopted. The Statutes of Wisconsin, Section 438, 1898, read:

> . . . shall contract with qualified teachers, specify in the contract the wages per week, month, or year to be paid, and when completed file the contract, with a copy of the certificate of the teacher so employed with the clerk.

A question arose under this statute [23] and the majority of the court held that this statute did not mean that a contract with a teacher had to be in writing. However, three judges dissented strongly to the decision and asked the majority of the court to explain just how an oral contract could be filed with the clerk of the school district, as the statute demanded. A later case reversed the above ruling.[24]

North Carolina has a statute requiring all contracts for the erection of buildings made by the board of education of a county to be in writing. A board of education having a building several miles from an electric power line desired to install this power in

[20] Midland Chemical Laboratories *v.* School District of Little Rock, 164 Ark. 38, 260 S. W. 726 (1924); Ryan *v.* Humphries, Okla. 150 P. 1107 (1925); Ruling Case Law, Vol. 24: 576–77, Sec. 25; 12 A. L. R. 25.

[21] Coberly *v.* Gainer, 69 W. Va. 699, 73 S. E. 790 (1911).

[22] Citizens State Bank *v.* School District No. 115, 124 Kan. 300, 259 P. 796 (1927).

[23] Pearson *v.* School District No. 8, Wis., 129 N. W. 940 (1911).

[24] Schaut *v.* Joint School District No. 6, Wis., 210 N. W. 270 (1926).

the building. It contracted with a party to build this line at a cost of $3,500 without putting the contract into writing and submitting the same for the approval of the State Superintendent of Public Instruction. The court held that the writing clause did not apply to contracts for lighting apparatus.[25]

Statutes of Missouri (Sec. 2164, Statutes 1919) requires all contracts with school districts to be in writing and hence a school district cannot be held liable on *quantum meruit* or any sort of an implied contract.[26]

The court in this case further stated:

. . . he and every other person dealing with a school board must be held to know that he cannot make a contract with a school district, except by complying with the statute and putting the contract in writing as the statute provides it must be done. When he takes any other course, he does so at his own risk.

In Illinois a written contract is not necessary,[27] while in Michigan[28] it was held that a supplementary contract orally agreed upon, and which modified a building contract, need not be in writing under a statute requiring all building contracts to be in writing.

Business practice today would seem to indicate that contracts with public bodies and corporations should be in writing. School business affairs have expanded rapidly. It is only good business practice to reduce agreements to a writing. This is absolutely necessary, if misunderstandings are to be avoided as to the nature and authorization of the expenditure. The writing furnishes to both parties and to all interested citizens a record in exact terms as to the nature of the transaction. Members of school boards and their officials are usually men of affairs, and why should they run the risk of misunderstanding, imposition, or even of possible charges of fraud or collusion, by not reducing the matters of detail to a writing. Writing itself is conducive to exactness and clearness of thinking, and understanding. Many times undertakings are abandoned or modified in important aspects after they have been reduced to a written instrument. The consideration necessary to formulate a binding and comprehensive contract brings to the surface many ramifications and possible complications

[25] Conrad *v.* Board of Education, N. C. 130 S. E. 53 (1925).
[26] Metz *v.* Warrick *et al.*, 217 Mo. A 504, 269 S. W. 626 (1925).
[27] Llewellyn *v.* Cicero Board of Education, 324 Ill. 254, 154 N. E. 889 (1926).
[28] Lather *v.* School District, 243 Mich. 90, 219 N. W. 700 (1928).

which might arise under such an agreement. Prudent men desire to think things through before committing themselves to important agreements. It seems that public officers or bodies should follow this practice. The proposed code requires (Article VIII, section 5) this type of formal action.

The statutory requirements concerning the administration of contracts are very meager in most states. Where the statutes are detailed, they usually concern some one type of contract, or some specific formality required. It is somewhat common to find elaborate code provisions concerning contracts for buildings,[29] teachers' contracts,[30] contracts for textbooks, and transportation. It is contended by this investigator that the items and details which shall go into contracts of all types can be handled much better by administrative regulation than by statutory regulation. The criteria cited in Chapter III would properly delegate the regulation to administrative officers because the distinction between what is lawful and what is unlawful is largely a matter of discretion. Under the plan of control developed here the State Board of Education will set up standards for the guidance of boards of education in these matters.[31] The proposed code also places state supervision over the form and legality of all contracts by making the State Commissioner of Education responsible for the formulation of legal forms of contracts [32] and also by appointing him the ultimate appeal tribunal to settle questions arising to their form.[33]

The law of contracts is a very complicated affair. It would be an herculean task even to enumerate the different problems which have arisen in the making, execution, and interpretation of contracts. In general, the school districts are subject to the same rights and liabilities under contracts as are other bodies and individuals. There is a tendency on the part of the courts to interpret public contracts a little more strictly than private contracts, especially those which concern the formalities of action and procedure required. Where the board of education does not have power to act, many times the parties with whom it has con-

---

[29] Henzlik, F. E., *Rights and Liabilities of Public School Boards Under Capital Outlay Contracts.*

[30] Allen, I. M., *The Teacher's Contractual Status.* Anderson, E. W., *The Teacher's Contract and Other Legal Phases of Teacher Status.*

[31] See Proposed Code, Art. IV, sec. 2.

[32] See Proposed Code, Art. V, sec. 1, subdiv. 5.

[33] See Proposed Code, Art. V, sec. 2, subdiv. 2g.

tracted have had to suffer. There is no need to build up a separate field of interpretation of contracts for the field of education, and it seems a sign of weakness for school boards to ask for immunities under contracts which could not be granted to private parties dealing in similar situations. Students desiring to study the rights and liabilities under contracts should consult some such standard treatise on contracts as the five-volume compendium written by Williston.[34]

The question of implied contracts and the ratification of contracts which are both matters of the administration of an expenditure program will be treated very briefly. These are very technical matters and the general rules only will be stated and illustrated.

Implied Contracts

III. The general rule is that contracts will not be implied as against a school board.[35]

One of the strongest pronouncements of this doctrine was made in Wisconsin:

> The facts from which a contract will be implied against a municipal corporation are quite different from those which raise an implication of contract between natural persons. It is a general rule that no contract will be implied against a municipality, if such implication would conflict with the statute prescribing a mode of contracting by which alone the municipality may bind itself.[36]

There have been several exceptions in cases usually involving claims for services already rendered or materials used and awards of damages given upon the theory of *quantum meruit.* The reasoning usually followed in this type of a case is similar to that stated by a Colorado judge as follows:

> The circumstances are such that the law independently of an express contract imposes an obligation upon the defendant district to do justice in respect to the benefits derived.[37]

Ratification of Contracts

IV. When a contract has been made by a board of education and it is afterwards found that it is unauthorized for some reason, the courts have not formulated any settled rules concerning the right of the board to ratify the contract. It is generally upheld that an illegal contract cannot be ratified.

[34] Williston, Samuel, *The Law of Contracts;* 5 vols.

[35] McQuillan, Eugene, *Municipal Corporations*, sec. 1495; Cyc. vol. 35, p. 964.

[36] School District No. 4 *v.* Industrial Commission, 194 Wis. 342, 216 N. W. 844 (1917).

[37] Mountjoy & Frewen *v.* Cheyenne Co. School District, 78 Colo. 165, 240 P. 464 (1925).

Judge Robbins of the Oklahoma Supreme Court stated the conflict of authority in this field:

In this connection it may not be out of place to say that the question of the power of municipal or quasi-municipal corporations to ratify unauthorized contracts is one of the generally recognized controversies of the court and bar. The authorities are absolutely irreconcilable: and after careful study of the proposition, the writer hereof acknowledges himself at sea, in the midst of storm and high rolling waves of uncertainty; but we gather from the weight of authorities that, where the corporation had power to enter into the contract under consideration, and the manner of making it being the only question involved, such contract may, as a rule, be ratified by an acceptance of the benefits of the contract by corporations and by subsequent recognition and substantial performance of the acts and conditions required by law in the execution of the legal contract by acquiescence in the conditions and benefits obtained by virtue of the contract.[38]

A general rule, however, is stated in the case of Miller *v.* Alsbaugh, "that ratification must be as formal as required in the execution of the original contract." [39]

An illegal contract cannot be ratified.[40]

Rights and Liabilities Under Statutes Requiring That Certain Contracts Be Let Only After Public Notice

V. Statutes requiring that contracts, under certain restrictions, must be awarded only after notice and a call for proposals or bids will be strictly enforced. An important exception is that contracts for personal service are usually not held to be within the requirement.

The law makes no distinction with respect to contracts under the control of the board of education and those made by other public bodies under the same or similar statutes. The administration of the expenditure power is and has been regulated rather strictly in various jurisdictions. The law reports are full of cases involving this phase of statutory regulation. This study will limit itself to a study of some of the more important phases of the statutes limiting the power of the boards of education, and will refer to legal authorities who have gathered together many decisions upon this topic.

The general rule showing the absolute requirement that "bids" must be called for as the statute directs is well stated by the

[38] Ryan *v.* Humphries, 500 Okla. 343, 150 P. 1106 (1915).

[39] Miller *v.* Alsbaugh, Mo. 2 S. W. 2nd 208 (1928).

[40] Shonk Land Co. *v.* Joachim *et al.*, 96 W. Va. 708, 129 S. E. 444 (1924).

Pennsylvania courts. The decision rendered after quoting the statute reads:

> . . . The use of the word "shall" leaves no room for the exercise of either option or discretion on the part of the board, in so far as contracts exceeding the amount are concerned. Courts have uniformly held provisions in the statutes requiring the obtaining of competitive bids for municipal and other public improvements to be mandatory, calling for strict compliance on the part of municipal officers.[41]

Exceptions to the General Rule

In the discussion of this topic, the exceptions are more important than the general rule. It is here that the trouble arises. The statute not being definite enough to allow certain discretion on the part of the board encourages it to go ahead and contract anyway, hoping that the court will make the same kind of exceptions as have been made in other jurisdictions. The most important of the exceptions allowed by the courts concern those contracts for personal service. The courts have excepted, in various jurisdictions, the following types of service from the statute: physicians, attorneys, architects, surveyors, engineers, accountants, stenographers, inspectors for new buildings, and common labor. A very complete list of cases involving this point may be found in the *American Law Reports* (1926), Vol. 44, beginning at page 1,150. The law therein quoted is the authority for the statements made in this paragraph.

The proposed code eliminates the cause of many of these cases as it definitely provides that all personal service shall not be held to come under the statutory provision.[42]

Formalities Required

Advertising and Specifications. Advertising for proposals or bids should be made in the name of the board of education and not by a committee.[43]

The specifications must be in "such form as to furnish a standard for real competitive bidding upon a uniform and intelligent basis." [44] It has also been held that "the printed form for bids should be read as part of the notice to bidders."[45]

[41] Appeal of Stout *et al.*, 258 Pa. 575, 102 A. 278 (1917).
[42] Proposed Code, Art. VIII, sec. 6, subdiv. a.
[43] Bauman *v.* City West Allis, 187 Wis., 506, 204 N. W. 907 (1925).
[44] Warnock *v.* Wray, 194 N. Y. S. 396 (1922).
[45] Maloney *v.* Maddever *et al.*, 136 N. Y. S. 498 (1912).

Discretion Allowed Board of Education Under Statutes Requiring Bids

VI. When a statute directs that the contract "shall be awarded to the lowest bidder," the courts are inclined to interpret this statute strictly. However, if the language is less mandatory the courts will usually allow the board some discretion in awarding the contract.

The language directing how the board shall act in awarding contracts varies. The bidder to whom the contract is to be awarded is described as:

"Lowest responsible"
"Lowest and best"
"Lowest reliable and responsible"
"Lowest"
"Responsible bidder offering the most advantageous terms"
"Persons presenting the most favorable proposal"
"Persons offering to perform contract at lowest price."[46]

The use of such words as "responsible," "reliable," "best," etc., are usually interpreted as allowing the board to exercise discretion in making the award, and that the board need not necessarily contract with the lowest bidder. The law on this subject is very complex and those interested in this particular phase of the law may find the evidence supporting the general statements made herein by inspecting *Lawyers' Reports Annotated*, Vol. 38, beginning at page 672, which discusses all the elements concerning the ability of the contractor which may be considered when the statute allows discretion on the part of the board in awarding the contract. This study will simply list the elements which the courts have considered, and which are reported in the references cited above.

"Ability and capacity"
"Bond, its sufficiency and substantial matter of form"
"Capital"
"Character and reputation of contractor"
"Competency and efficiency"
"Energy"
"Experience"
"Facilities"
"Faithfulness and fidelity"

[46] Definitions of each of these terms may be read in *Annotated Cases*, 1913A, p. 497.

"Fraud or unfairness in previous contract"
"General qualifications"
"Good faith"
"Honesty"
"Integrity"
"Judgment"
"Laxity in previous dealings"
"Promptness"
"Quality of previous work"
"Reliability and trustworthiness"
"Skill"
"Suitability to particular task"

Recent cases uphold the liberal interpretation of this discretionary authority.[47]

ATTEMPTED EVASIONS OF THE STATUTES REQUIRING "BIDS"

One evasion of the statute requiring bids is the award of several separate contracts, each for a sum less than the amount prescribed by statute, but the total of which is clearly in excess of the statutory limitation. This type of evasion has been condemned:

> The present case turned on whether the purchase of the stoves constituted one or two transactions. . . . While the evidence for the petitioners tended to show that the stoves were ordered as a single transaction, and that the making of the written orders separate was a subterfuge to cover up the real transaction so that each contract would indicate an expenditure of less than $300 and apparently be within the law.[48]

The board of directors in this case were removed for entering into such a contract even though the transaction was never consummated.

One of the most subtle ways of evasion and also the means of collusion on the part of contracting parties is the making of supplementary contracts or agreements. The cases involving current expenses are relatively few in this field. There are a few cases involving this principle which concern building contracts which will apply with equal force to any other contract of a board of education. There are two decisions from important jurisdictions which are opposed in principle. The Pennsylvania decision would not allow changes which eliminated the penalty clause and

[47] Ellingson *v.* Cherry Lake School District, 55 N. D. 141, 212 N. W. 773 (1927); Flynn Construction Co. *v.* Leininger, Okla. 257, P. 378 (1927).

[48] Petition of Murray *et al.*, 262 Pa. 188, 105 A. 61 (1918).

the requirement that the contractor carry workmen's compensation insurance from the contract after the award.[49]

The New York courts allowed the New York City Board of Education to make a supplementary agreement with a heating and ventilating contractor for a sum of $62,000 as extra cost when the contractor was delayed by reasons beyond his control. The court said:

> . . . Agreement to continue work under contract held not a new contract, which could not be entered into without bids.[50]

The fact that neither of these cases has been cited, nor overruled, is an indication of the fewness of such disputes involving this principle in the courts. The fact that the use of supplementary agreements may be conducive to collusion and fraud are reasons why the proposed code is so developed as to obviate such possibilities.[51]

It has been held that a board of education is not justified in awarding a contract without bids because of a reason given that the time necessary for the securing of bids would delay the opening of school.[52]

When Must Bids Be Considered?

A school board is entitled to a reasonable time to determine which bid is the lowest and most reasonable.[53]

Is Statutory Requirement of Public Bids Justified?

Buckalew reports that twenty-two states require that contracts be let only after receiving of bids, and that the minimum amounts which may be contracted without bids ranges from $50 to $500.[54] Taylor,[55] after a thorough study made of this phase of school purchasing, establishes this policy of letting contracts after notice and bids as one of the criteria of an efficient purchasing plan. He excepts only perishable articles. Taylor found that all of the fourteen large business enterprises whose purchasing

[49] Lehigh Coal and Navigation Co. *v.* Summitt Hill School District, 137 A. 140, 289 Pa. 75 (1927).

[50] Wells & Newton *v.* Craig, 133 N. Y. 419 (1921).

[51] See Proposed Code, Art. VIII, sec. 6, subdiv. b.

[52] Appeal of Stout *et al.*, 258 Pa. 575, 102 A. 278 (1917).

[53] People *v.* Board of Education New York City, 188 N. Y. S. 686 (1921).

[54] Buckalew, H. L., "Purchase of School Supplies," *American School Board Journal*, 74: 66–70 J. '27.

[55] Taylor, R. B., *Principles of School Supply Management*, pp. 12–13.

policies were studied secured bids before letting contracts. The fact that these commercial enterprises find it good business practice should be rather conclusive evidence that the practice should be followed in other business enterprises.[56]

Buck [57] advocates the solicitation of bids by cities as a part of their purchasing plan.

The proposed code, Article VIII, section 6, is drawn to insure this method of securing honesty and economy in the administration of expenditure programs. The code sections covering this control of expenditures are so developed as to avoid the weaknesses of the codes herein mentioned now commonly regulating this item of administration.

PERSONAL PECUNIARY INTEREST OF BOARD MEMBERS AND SCHOOL OFFICIALS IN EXPENDITURES

VII. The courts interpret strictly statutes which prohibit personal financial interest of board members or school officials in contracts made for the school district. The common law, in the absence of statute, prohibits such interest.

Thirty-five states prohibit any pecuniary interest on the part of a board member in any contract made on behalf of the board of education. Eleven states forbid the hiring of relatives of board members to teach or occupy other offices. The common law has always held that public officers must not have any personal pecuniary interest in their own acts as public officials. The statutory requirements, therefore, indicate a desire more clearly to define the nature of the interest prohibited. The question arises as to how to do this, and this calls for an examination of the courts' decisions with reference to this matter in order to determine how far the courts will enforce such a provision.

A member of the board of education of the city of Akron, in 1894, sold to the board of education, of which he was a member, goods to the value of $29.09. Judge Varis discusses the principles involved in the following manner: [58]

> The dollar and cent advantage is the lowest order of consideration that can be urged, when a public wrong, a vicious public example is encouraged under

[56] *Ibid.*, 136–45. The companies studied were: Corn Exchange Bank, Western Union, American Express (Banking Division), Atlantic and Pacific Stores, Chatham and Phoenix Bank, Metropolitan Life Insurance Co., Equitable Life Assurance Co., Irving Trust Company, Columbia University, New York Central Lines, American Railway Express, United Cigar Co., New York Life Insurance Co., and New York Post Office.

[57] Buck, A. E., *Municipal Finance*, p. 266.

[58] Grant *v.* Brouse, 1 Ohio Nisi Prius 145.

high official sanction; for example, the public wrong, the prostitution of public virtue is vastly more than a mere matter of dollars and cents. The law was made in the interests of sound public policy and, while in some cases it may appear to be more advantageous to ignore than to obey the law, yet we think no public officer can violate a direct provision of law, directing the performance of his duty, or prohibiting certain acts, and have his conduct judicially approved. And where the matter comes before this court, it ought carefully to see to it that public policy is upheld. I know of no better way of preserving the virtue of the public than to have its officers understand and act as if they were public servants, always recognizing that official position constitutes a public trust that must be sacredly carried out.

A concise statement of recent date summarizes the law today:[59]

It is an inexorable rule of the common law, and it finds expression in our statute that public servants shall not be interested directly or indirectly in any contract made with public agencies of which they are members. Public service demands an exclusive fidelity. The law tolerates no mingling of self-interest.

The principle of prohibiting a personal interest on the part of board members has been upheld in numerous jurisdictions. The most illuminating cases will come, therefore, from the borderline cases where the distinction is not quite so clear.

A board of education may not contract with the husband of a lady director for the transportation of pupils to and from school, nor may the board contract with a "hired man" of the family who uses the family conveyances to transport children.[60]

In the case of Keenon *v.* Adams, the court held that a sub-district trustee may not contract or expend money for the board in making repairs and furnishing supplies to the school, but that he may legally contract for the transportation of children.[61] The court's reasoning was that transportation was not definitely mentioned in the statute prohibiting self-interest but the supplies, buildings, and equipment were. These transportation cases are rather interesting as some few of the states definitely exempt transportation from the statutory rule. This is done for the reason that it is sometimes difficult in rural districts to secure any disinterested party to undertake the contract. It is sometimes almost impossible to secure anyone to make minor repairs upon a school building in rural districts. This type of contract is sometimes exempt from the statutory and common-law rule.

---

[59] Ames *v.* Board of Education, Montclair, N. J. 127 A. 95 (1925).

[60] Directors School District No. 30 *v.* Libby, 135 Wash. 233, 237 P. 505 (1925).

[61] Keenon *v.* Adams, Ky. 196, S. W. 173 (1917).

A less rigid rule is found in Arkansas where a contract made by a board with one of its members is not absolutely void, but only voidable.[62] In New York, when a member of the board agreed to work for a contractor at $1.00 per hour, as supervisor of the work upon a school building, it was held that the contract was not binding but that money already paid could not be recovered.[63] Indiana is more severe. A person having a contract with the board of education which is not complete at the time of his election to the board may not recover the balance due on the contract.[64]

Personal Interest of Employees of the Board

The prohibition of personal pecuniary interest in any contract or expenditure of the board (other than in his own contract of employment) on the part of any employee of the board is likewise forbidden in a few states. The reasoning of the courts in the cases involving pecuniary interest of the board members applies with equal force to this type of interest. The only exceptions which appear to be justified concern necessary expenses for transportation in the pursuance of an officer's duties, and possibly contracts for janitor's service in rural districts, where it is sometimes impossible to get another to contract for such service. A Kentucky court in 1916 would not permit a county superintendent to charge the board for the use of his horse and the use of a buggy belonging to his brother, in order to carry out the duties of the position.[65] A county superintendent may not build a schoolhouse for the board of education,[66] nor may he employ his wife to fill the position as supervisor.[67]

This prohibition of personal pecuniary interest of board members or school officials in the contracts which they have to execute is essentially sound. It is provided that such interest be prohibited in the proposed code.[68]

There have been occasional cases where the board of education has been prohibited from contracting for services or from expend-

---

[62] Smith *v.* Danridge *et al.*, 98 Ark. 83 W., 135 S. (800) 1911.

[63] Ryszka *v.* Board of Education, 214 N. Y. S. 264, 126 Misc. Rep. 622 (1926).

[64] Noble *v.* Davidson, 177 Ind. 19, 96 N. E. 325 (1911).

[65] Beauchamp *v.* Taylor, Ky. 185 S. W. 868 (1916).

[66] Farmers and Merchants National Bank *v.* School District No. 56, 35 Okla. 506, 130 P. 549 (1913).

[67] Neilson *v.* Richards County Auditor, 75 Cal. A. 680, 243 P. 697 (1926)

[68] Proposed Code, Art. VIII, sec. 8.

ing funds outside the school district. Such cases usually involve contracts for transportation or for coöperative services rendered by a school nurse, physician, or other desirable types of service. Such prohibitions many times may keep a school district from establishing some such service, which it could not have if it had to finance the project alone. Lack of such power might also prevent districts from coöperating in putting up a high school building or conducting a joint consolidated school. Therefore, a positive power is given to the boards of education under Article VIII, section 12, in the proposed code, to make any such coöperative contracts.

The provisions of Article VIII, section 13, are inserted in order to fix the responsibility for all acts involving the expenditure of money. This is necessary in order to have a written record of the vote, so, in case of violation of the law, the evidence is there to fix the responsibility.

CHAPTER VIII

OTHER LEGAL CONTROLS FOR THE PURPOSE OF INSURING HONESTY AND EFFICIENCY IN THE ADMINISTRATION OF EXPENDITURES

Warrants, Accounting, Audit, Reporting, and Personal Liability of Individual Board Members

The following matters relating to other legal controls of the administration of expenditures are to be discussed in this chapter:

I. In the absence of a specific statute, the power to authorize the issuance of warrants cannot be delegated by the board of education.

II. The statutes of the several states are diverse and incomplete as to the form and subject matter which a school warrant should contain. Neither the law of the courts nor the statutes furnish any clear criteria for determining the rules which should govern the issuance of warrants.

III. The statutes of the several states, in most instances, permit warrants to be issued when funds are not available to pay the same.

IV. Warrants ordinarily have been held by the courts to have the right to priority of payment in the order of presentation. However, statutes requiring registration in order to establish priority will be strictly enforced.

V. Warrants issued by a school board have all the attributes of negotiability, except that of freedom from original defenses.

VI. Money paid out illegally by a board of education can be recovered in most jurisdictions, but the courts are confused when called upon to restore money paid out by mistake of law.

VII. The general rule is that no external body or official shall be allowed to pass upon matters other than the form, correctness of the account, or compliance with the statutory standards.

VIII. Each of the states require some form of accounts to be kept by each school district. The nature of the accounts required varies from the simple requirement that accounts be kept to a highly centralized and mandatory state system.

IX. The statutory requirement of an audit of accounts of local school districts is provided for by the laws of most states. The requirements vary all the way from an audit by the board itself or by a committee of citizens to a real professional audit by the state.

X. The statutes of most of the states require that some form of publicity be given to the expenditure program of the board of education. These statutes are usually very indefinite.

XI. Taxpayers will generally be successful in enjoining the action of a board of education when they question the legality of the board's action, but they will not be successful when questioning the discretionary powers of the board.

XII. Statutes imposing individual personal liability upon the members of boards of education and their officers for unlawfully expending money have been upheld rather strictly by the courts.

Authorization of Issuance of Warrants

I. In the absence of a specific statute, the power to authorize the issuance of warrants cannot be delegated by the board of education.

The terms "warrant," "voucher," "order," and "check" are each used in the law reports, in different jurisdictions, to name the same thing. In legal terminology, any of these terms may be used to designate an order legally issued by a body or an officer having the power to issue the same upon an officer having charge of funds to pay out the same in accordance with such order. In this section the term "warrant" will be used and may be understood to represent any order of the board of education or its legally authorized agent to pay out funds upon presentation of the warrant. The general rule is:

> Warrants can only be issued by order of the board, and we do not understand that the board, even when acting as a board, can bind its members to make certain specified action on any question that may come before them.[1]

A leading Iowa case is equally definite that the board itself must audit and allow claims and that this power cannot be delegated to any other person or officer.[2] This case was upheld in

[1] Miller *v.* Alsbaugh, Mo., 2 S. W. 2nd 208 (1928).

[2] Heath *v.* Allbrook, 123 Iowa 559, 98 N. W. 619 (1904).

1926.[3] Where a treasurer disburses money improperly without the consent of the board, the board members cannot be held responsible for such illegal disbursement.[4]

A different rule holds in Wisconsin[5] where the executive committee of the board, acting for the board, may issue orders or warrants. Kansas[6] permits board members to bind the board by signing warrants individually. The designation of the county superintendent as the issuing power, without submission of the warrants to the board of supervisors, was upheld when applied to teachers' salaries in Mississippi.[7] In Nevada,[8] the county superintendent may issue orders upon the county auditor without the approval of the county commissioners, but the county commissioners may act as a board of appeal in case of disputed bills.

An examination of the statutes reveals the fact that the states have been very loath to delegate the authorization of the issuance of warrants to administrative officers. There are still thirty-one states which designate by statute that the board of education shall order the warrants issued. In four states the county superintendent may issue warrants under certain conditions, while in three states the director or township trustee has this power. There is not a single state which allows a city superintendent or business manager to issue warrants for goods received or salaries due.

Legal Requisites Before the Issuance of Warrants

II. The statutes of the several states are diverse and incomplete as to the form and subject matter of school warrants. Neither the law of the courts nor the law of the statutes furnish any clear criteria for determining the rules which should govern the issuance of warrants.

The statutes have attempted to insure honesty in the disbursement of money by establishing certain safeguards in the issuance of warrants or orders. The most usual custom is to have some official sign the order to pay. There is a great variety of officials designated to do this ministerial act. The most usual set of officials to be required to sign are the president or chairman of the

[3] Rural District Eagle *v.* Daly, 201 Iowa 286, 207 N. W. 124 (1926).

[4] State *v.* Julian, 93 Ind. 292.

[5] Rogers-Ruger Co. *v.* Board of Directors, Brule, Wis. 120, N. W. 849 (1909).

[6] Citizens State Bank *v.* School District No. 115, 124 Kan. 300, 259 P. 796 (1927).

[7] State *v.* Queen County Superintendent, 111 Miss. 32, 71 So. 171 (1911).

[8] Whittaker and Ray Co. *v.* Roberts, 155 F. 882 (1907).

board together with the clerk or secretary; eighteen states make this a positive requirement. The clerk or secretary alone signs in five states and the president or chairman in three. The county superintendent signs in three states, the director and clerk in two states. Other persons designated to sign warrants in at least one state are county auditor, township trustee, director, whoever designated by the board, school committee certified by the superintendent, selectmen, moderator, trustee.

Certain formalities are required in an effort to insure that the board is securing full value for the funds expended and the statutory requirements are exceedingly interesting. An examination of the school codes, in the thirty states making requirements as to what facts a warrant must show, gives considerable information as to the confused ideas which legislatures seem to think will secure an honest and accurate administration of the payment of funds. The facts are as follows:

Requirements that Warrant Must Show	Number of States Making Requirement
Fund on which drawn	9
Itemized bill	9
Verification under oath	7
Purpose	6
Payee	5
Consideration	4
Date	3
Amount	3
Receipt required	3
Certified correct	2
Written	2
Address of payee	1
Certified unpaid	1
Approved by superintendent	1
Order to be paid	1
That competitive bids were called for if over $100 in amount	1
Payroll must be sworn to by superintendent	1
Payroll must show certificate of civil service commission that persons are employed and entitled to salary to be paid	1
Designate fiscal year in which paid	1
Bill must be filed 30 days before payment	1
Be on a special blank	1

These requirements are all the more interesting when it is considered that eighteen states make no regulations at all and some of the states included in the statement above make several of the requirements shown. These facts show the very great inadequacy of the regulations of this important matter. It is quite evident that there has been little thought given to this detail. The legislatures have adopted what occurred to them to be good ideas in protecting school funds from unlawful administration. One can easily see the amount of detail which would have to go into a statute properly to regulate the administration of the issuance of warrants.

It was thought that an examination of the court decisions upon cases involving payment of warrants would help clarify our ideas upon this subject, but few cases were found which had the formality of issue as the point in question. This is some evidence that the formalities of issue may not be the fundamental considerations in safeguarding expenditures. There is, of course, another reason why cases do not arise in this field of law and that is that troubles ordinarily arise before the warrant is issued, and, should the warrant be found faulty after the payee receives his money, there is not much likelihood of a suit.

This lack of common standards and, consequently, diverse statutes is another illustration of the futility of attempting to regulate something which determines details of ministerial action without having the same reduced to scientific standards. It would appear that there is opportunity for a study in business management to determine just what are the essential procedures in this field of school administration.

Under criterion II, as stated by Freund, the legislature should not attempt specifically to regulate matters for which no definite standards are available and therefore the proposed code[9] delegates the power to the state board of education to determine the details of this item of administration of the expenditure program.

Issuance of Warrants When Funds Are Not Available for Their Payment

III. The statutes of the several states in most instances permit warrants to be issued when funds are not available to pay the same.

[9] Proposed Code, Art. IV, sec. 2, subdiv. f, g, h, and j.

Nevada, Pennsylvania, Rhode Island, South Carolina, and Virginia will not allow warrants to be issued except when funds are available to pay such indebtedness. New York makes the requirement that funds must be on hand before orders to pay teachers' salaries are issued. In eighteen states [10] it is either implied or definitely stated that funds need not be on hand, while in the other twenty-four states nothing is said. These states finance a considerable portion of their school program by means of warrants which may, upon fulfilling certain prerequisites, become evidences of indebtedness.

The issuance of warrants before funds are available, which thus creates a floating debt of the district, is a rather questionable practice.[11] Unless such a procedure is carefully regulated, it is impossible to keep boards of education within the limits of their estimated income. It is also exceedingly difficult to get at the exact financial status of the school district. The practice may also lead to a depreciation of the obligations of the district and to discounting of warrants at heavy rates in order to secure funds.

A Kansas school board did follow this practice and discounted its warrants for as much as 50% of their face value.[12] The practice is even more to be condemned when teachers and other employees who have rendered services or persons who have delivered goods have to stand the loss necessary when warrants have to be discounted.

Payment of Warrants

IV. Warrants ordinarily have been held by the courts to have the right to priority of payment in the order of presentation. However, statutes requiring registration in order to establish priority will be strictly enforced.

Warrants should be paid in the order of their presentation, and the treasurer has no right to hold funds for the payment of any particular obligations.[13] Registration of warrants, however, is required by statute in many states in order to establish priority of payment and a condition precedent to a suit upon the warrant.[14]

---

[10] Ariz., Ark., Colo., Idaho, Iowa, Kan., Ky., Mass., Mont., Neb., N. J., N. C., N. D., Ohio, Okla., Ore., S. D., and Wash.

[11] Lutz, H. L., *Public Finance*, p. 545.

[12] Home State Bank *v.* School District No. 17, Kan. 169 P. 202 (1917).

[13] Reed *v.* People, 34 Wyo. 163, 242 P. 319 (1926).

[14] Crawford Treas. *v.* Brisley, 131 Okla. 230, 268 P. 713 (1928).

It would seem that a treasurer before paying a warrant would require an order or other regularly issued evidence originating with legally constituted officers before paying out any money. There are several cases, however, where moneys have been paid out without an order. A case had to be decided in (Duluth) Minnesota last year. In this case the Peoples Bank originally held some warrants and assigned them to another bank. The treasurer paid the Peoples Bank money which was intended to be in payment of one of the outstanding warrants, but the treasurer did not demand and receive the warrant. The board was required to pay the original warrant.[15]

Negotiability of Warrants

V. Warrants issued by a school board have all the attributes of negotiability, except that of freedom from original defenses.

The general rule as to the negotiability of school warrants is stated in the case of First National Bank Duluth *v.* School District No. 17, Carlton, *supra,*

> We take judicial notice of the fact that from very early days, while municipal warrants have never been negotiable, they have been transferable by indorsement and delivery and have been treated by banks and dealers in commercial páper as having all the attributes of negotiability, except that of freedom from original defenses.

An earlier case, that of Boardman *v.* Hayne (1870),[16] states the rule which to all intents and purposes was not changed in the Duluth case.

> A school order, drawn upon the treasurer of a district township, by the president and secretary, is not a negotiable instrument, and the assignee thereof takes it subject to all equities and defenses that it would have been subject to in the hands of the payee.

A warrant was issued for the payment of a carload of lumber before its delivery, and the lumber was never delivered. A Mississippi court held this to be a negligent act on the part of the board, but would not allow payment of the warrant even though it was in the hands of an innocent third party.[17]

Numerous other cases might be cited which uphold this theory as to the non-negotiability of school warrants. Students desiring

---

[15] First National Bank Duluth *v.* School District No. 17, Carlton, 173 Minn. 383, 217 N. W. 366 (1928).

[16] Boardman *v.* Hayne, 29 Iowa 339.

[17] Reese *v.* Isola State Bank, Miss. 105 So. 636 (1926).

further information on this subject and citations of many cases will find much information of value in A. L. R., Vol. 36, p. 949. This brings together all the important cases on this subject decided prior to 1925.

It might well be questioned in the light of present organization of the business of a school system why this special rule is needed for the protection of the board. Why should school boards pay a claim in the first place if it is not legal in every particular? Why should the law allow school boards to be "Indian Givers"? Perhaps a partial answer will be found in a consideration of those cases where a board of education has recovered money when illegally paid out.

Recovery of Money Paid Out Illegally or by Mistake

VI. Money paid out illegally by a board of education can be recovered in most jurisdictions, but the courts are confused when called upon to restore money paid out by mistake of law.

Where the treasurer pays out money illegally, he or his bondsmen can be held liable for such funds.[18] A board may revoke its order to pay if induced by fraud or mistake.[19] Money paid by mistake of law may be recovered by a board of education.[20] The court in the syllabus of this case said:

> Rule that money paid by mistake of law may not be recovered does not apply to unauthorized disbursement of public funds; action may be maintained to recover public funds paid without authority, although paid by mistake of law.

This case involved the payment of money by a school district to a community high school for tuition of pupils residing in the plaintiff district. The district paid the tuition but, after its payment, discovered that under the statute the county commissioners should have paid it from county funds. The board was successful in maintaining its action. This law is the exact opposite of what it is in private cases.

Where funds were erroneously distributed to and consumed in educational purposes in another district, such funds cannot be recovered.[21]

---

[18] School District No. 45 *v.* Correll, 220 Mo. App. 322, 286 S. W. 136 (1926).

[19] Somerville *v.* Wood, 115 Ala. 534, 22 So. 476 (1897).

[20] School District No. 49 *v.* Community High School, 126 Kan. 51, 267 P. 23 (1928).

[21] Carter Special School District *v.* Hollis Special School District, 173 Ark. 781, 293 S. W. 722 (1927).

A rule, which may prove interesting and which is applicable to many situations, concerns the right to hold money belonging to a party with whom the board is contracting, if other money has already been paid out illegally.[22] This rule is especially applicable to building contracts and to any continuing type of contract.

When public money has been paid without authority of law, and the public official has money of the recipient in his hands, he is not compelled to pay such money over and sue to recover the illegal payments, but may hold, subject to the decision of the court when the claimant sues, and thus avoid a multiplicity of suits.

Audit of Bills as a Control of Expenditures

VII. The general rule is that no external body or official shall be allowed to pass upon matters other than the form, correctness of the account, or compliance with statutory standards.

One of the most mooted questions with reference to the control of expenditures especially in fiscally dependent cities is the control which the auditor, comptroller or controller exercises over the expenditures of the board of education. The general rule was stated concisely by Judge Davis of the New York Court of Appeals:

The provisions of the law . . . requiring the counter-signature of the commissioner of finance and accounts on the warrant, and requiring the board to classify its funds and furnish data to the financial officers of the city, is merely to enable that officer to keep an account of the disbursements, and an additional protection to insure compliance with statutory requirements and the genuineness of the audit by the board of education.[23]

The reasons for denying the power were stated in New York to be:

If the latter board (Board of Estimate) by the form of its appropriations could require such an audit or approval, the control of these matters would soon pass to the board of estimate, and the whole purpose of the Education Law be subverted.[24]

This principle was upheld in Texas in 1928.[25]

The act of the comptroller is held to be ministerial, and, so long as the claim is for a charge which is a proper one against the educational fund, he must issue the order.[26]

---

[22] Agnes Township *et al.* *v.* Grand Fork Co., 56 N. D. 505, 218 N. W. 212 (1928).
[23] Rief *v.* Schwab, 204 N. Y. App. 50 (1922).
[24] Brennan *v.* Board of Education, 245 N. Y. 8, 156 N. E. 78 (1927).
[25] Chrestman *v.* Thompkins, 5 S. W. 2nd 257, Texas (1928).
[26] People *v.* Craig, 223 N. Y. 125, 133 N. E. 419 (1921).

Accounting as a Control of Expenditures

VIII. Each of the states requires that some form of accounts be kept by each school district. The nature of the accounts required varies from the simple requirement that accounts be kept to a highly centralized and mandatory state system.

A very important control over the administration of expenditures is an accurate accounting for each and every item of expenditure. Good accounting practice tends to insure honesty and economy of expenditures, affords a check upon policies and plans, makes available information as to status of the expenditure budget at any particular time, and is a very important phase in aiding in the planning and administration of future expenditures.

Well-organized and complete systems of school accounting have been established in New York, New Jersey, Pennsylvania, and Idaho under the direction of the state department of education. Other states which have state systems of accounting for school funds directed by the department of education are Alabama, Arizona, and Rhode Island. Wisconsin and Michigan have state systems of accounting which have been adopted voluntarily by the local school districts. Iowa has a system which has been developed by the State Auditor and adopted in most of the districts. Ohio and Indiana have well-established and well-organized systems of uniform accounting under the direction of an accounting department which is not under the department of education. New Mexico has a state system under an official known as the Educational Budget Officer. The state auditor regulates the accounting in the schools of Connecticut and Washington. Massachusetts cities are under a Director of Accounts who is not in any way connected with the educational work as is the practice in Wyoming where the officer is called the State Examiner of Accounts. In New Hampshire the State Tax Commission regulates the accounting in the school districts. Since practically all of these school districts have developed this state regulation of accounting during the past ten years, there is a definite trend toward state supervision of accounting.

Cases concerning the accounting procedures of cities are very scarce in the law reports. Some were found but they do not involve the issues which seem most fundamental in this field and do not help toward a solution of the problem. Persons suing the school boards usually are after specific relief and, so long as they are able to prevail in the courts, do not bring up questions of accounting.

It is generally accepted that the accounting systems which produced the financial statistics of the past generation were not very effective. Comparable financial statistics are still exceedingly hard to obtain. The local communities did not and probably would not produce adequate accounting systems. As to whether the proper results can best be obtained by a statutory regulation or by administrative control is, therefore, the principal problem confronting school administrators.

Under the criteria suggested by Freund,[27] accounting becomes a proper subject of control by administrative action. The distinction between lawful and unlawful procedure in this field is sometimes very difficult to determine. This is shown by the inability of school men to agree upon a proper classification of the items of expenditure for school accounting purposes, and, even when agreed, to interpret the classification rules in the same manner. Many excellent systems of accounting have been developed, but their application to all types of districts is something still to be desired. Strayer and Haig [28] point out in Educational Finance Inquiry that there is little chance to develop proper budgetary and accounting procedure in the small districts, and maintain that larger units are necessary if efficiency is to be secured in these matters. The fact is that we still have and will have these small units with us for some time. Some form of accounting must be secured which these officers can and will follow. In the accounting systems mentioned herein, several states, such as New York, New Jersey, and Pennsylvania, have greatly improved the accounting procedure. The fact that the successful systems of uniform accounting have been developed by the state education departments with only general control by the legislature is proof that this is a matter for administrative action. It would be next to impossible to write a statute which would provide for flexibility and change which is needed in this type of administrative action.

Freund's criterion III directs that administrative action is proper where it is necessary and desirable to determine compliance

[27] *Ante*, p. 25.

[28] Strayer, G. D. and Haig, R. M., *Educational Finance Inquiry*, Vol. I, p. 187.

with the law. The state is certainly interested in knowing whether its funds have been used efficiently and honestly. It is also interested in knowing whether the funds which it contributes have been used for the purposes intended.

The proposed code, Article IV, section 2, places the power to regulate accounting in the hands of the State Department of Education. It should be noticed, however, that any state system established must take into account the knowledge and advice of the local school districts. The provisions are such that any district which thinks that it may improve upon the state system will still have the opportunity to experiment all it pleases, so long as it produces the information which the state demands. This should leave all the opportunity necessary for local initiative.

Audit of Accounts

IX. The statutory requirement of an audit of accounts of local school districts is provided for by the laws of most of the states. The requirements vary all the way from an audit by the board itself or a committee of citizens to a real professional audit by the state.

The states of Georgia, New Jersey, and New Mexico have in the State Department of Public Instruction a division which is to audit the financial accounts of the school districts of the state. Rhode Island has the power to establish such an audit. The states of Delaware, Indiana, Louisiana, Massachusetts, Ohio, Washington, and Wyoming have auditors authorized by other departments of the state government which are assigned the duty of auditing the accounts of all the school districts of the respective states. North Carolina and New Hampshire reserve the right to audit the accounts of school districts at any time, and in Arizona the State Superintendent may investigate the local accounts.

There is legal precedent as to the constitutionality of establishment of a state audit of accounts. The specific question involved was the requirement that local districts pay the cost of the audit when done by the state officials. In both the cases cited, the right of the state to impose the audit was attacked on the ground that the legislature was imposing a tax upon a local government. The right was upheld in both cases.[29]

No study has been made of the relative effectiveness of the audit

[29] State *v.* Burr, 65 Wash. 524, 118 P. 639 (1911); State *v.* Shumate, 75 Ohio State 487 (1905).

made by the state department of education and the audits made of educational finances by other departments of the state government. It is impossible, therefore, to draw any scientifically supported conclusions as to the efficiency of these two types of auditing procedures. Linn,[30] in his study, presents some strong arguments for the placing of this power and duty in the state department of education.

McQuillin, an eminent legal authority upon municipal government, concludes after discussing laws authorizing audits:

> . . . Laws seek to protect the public funds by preventing waste of public moneys, and to enable the members of the public to learn the financial condition of the local corporation that appropriate remedies, if needed, may be devised. Laws of this character are liberally construed to effectuate such intent.[31]

It is, therefore, reasonable to conclude that any state system of audit established would have a reasonable chance to be upheld by the courts.

The conclusions concerning audit follow somewhat closely the discussion and reasoning given for state control of accounting. The application of Freund's criteria would follow verbatim the arguments made to place accounting under state administrative control.[32]

There are some strong arguments for the inclusion of the audit under administrative control of the state department of education. (Criterias IV and V, as suggested by Freund, namely, the lack of standards and the fostering of experiments.) There are reasons to believe that the administration of a school audit is still in its infancy. Audit, as all too commonly used today, is simply a checking of the accuracy and authorization of financial affairs. So far school auditing practice has not usually checked the values received from the expenditures made. The state should be interested in knowing the amount and quality of service it is securing from its expenditures, not to say anything of the great need locally to know just what is accomplished. Let a simple illustration be given. In the budget the policy of the school is stated, that the average class in the grades is to be 40 pupils and in the high school 28 pupils. Who checks to see that this policy has been carried out? It is quite probable that some local or state

[30] Linn, H. H., *Safeguarding School Funds.*

[31] McQuillin, Eugene, *Municipal Corporations*, sec. 2317.

[32] *Ante*, p. 121ff.

officer will work out some method of carefully and quickly checking such policies in the terms of service rendered and report upon this to the public the same as to the honesty in the use of the money. This need is pointed out by Upson [33] in its relation to both budget making and auditing.

For these reasons it is clear that the audit should not be subject to statutory regulation, but left to administrative control. It should be pointed out that school administrators should examine with care the inroads which other state departments are making into this field of control. So far it has not been a restrictive control. It may become a very important control just as it has in England, where one of the principal controls exercised over finances is that of central audit.[34]

Publicity

X. The statutes of most of the states require that some form of publicity be given to the expenditure program of boards of education. These statutes are usually very indefinite.

Popular control over the expenditure program is recognized by practically all students of government and school administration as being extremely important under a democratic form of government. If this power of control is to be exercised in an intelligent manner, then complete, understandable reports respecting the policies, purposes, and results of the expenditure of public funds must be disseminated.

Statutory requirements are inadequate to secure such reports. The school official is rare who can prepare a brief, intelligible, complete, and readable report upon the school finances. There should be in this field every opportunity for individual initiative to develop the necessary procedures and types of material which should be given to the public. Therefore no definite prescriptions will be laid down in the proposed code. The code will simply require that at least one report be printed each year and that the State Commissioner of Education shall be the sole judge as to the adequacy of the report.[35]

There are fortunately other forms of reports than such an annual report. The budget is one form of such a report. The

[33] Upson, Lent D., "Half Time Budget Methods," *Annals, American Academy of Political and Social Science*, 113: 69–74, May, 1924.

[34] Ashley, Percy, *Local and Central Government*, p. 353.

[35] Proposed Code, Art. VIII, sec. 10, and Art. IV, sec. 2, subdiv. h.

provisions of the proposed code requiring a public hearing should contribute something to the solution of this problem. The public hearing will tend to educate the school officials as to the type of fiscal information in which the public may be interested. It will also force them to prepare financial information in such form that it can be understood by the ordinary citizen. Until such time as such information is available, there will be suspicion and unwarranted accusations of unnecessarily high expenditures. Such a hearing will also afford an opportunity for the board and the executive officers to educate the public as to some of the more complicated fiscal problems and policies.

That the books of the board of education should be open to interested citizens is regarded as a rather important requirement,[36] yet less than half of the states have such a provision upon the statute books. The Kentucky Court of Appeals states the reasons for such a statute very forcefully:

> . . . These provisions manifest a purpose on the part of the legislature that the acts of the county superintendent, as well as the board of education, shall be kept so that any ordinary citizen who may desire to question their accuracy, or for any other purposes, may have access to them. It cannot be imagined that it was intended by the legislature that the right of inspection of the books of the board of education by the citizens was intended only to gratify his curiosity. On the contrary, the purpose was that such inspection was given for revisory purposes, and if the discretion given to the board in the incurring of expenses had been abused, its actions in so doing might be reviewed. . . .[37]

In view of the facts that there are no available standards and that such standards can only be developed through the encouragement of a great amount of individual action and experimentation, this matter is very properly a matter of administrative control.

Public Control of Expenditures—Right of Taxpayers to Question Expenditures

XI. Taxpayers will generally be successful in enjoining the action of a board of education when they question the legality of the board's action, but they will not be successful when questioning the discretionary powers of the board.

Closely related to the problem of publicity is the question: What may a citizen do in case he discovers some illegal or dishon-

[36] See Proposed Code, Art. VIII, sec. 11.

[37] Beauchamp *v.* Snider, Ky. 185, S. W. 868 (1916).

est action on the part of the board? What are his rights under the law? A leading case defining the rights of those who may question expenditures is that of Noble *v.* Davidson.[38]

> It has been held repeatedly by this court that one or more resident taxpayers of a municipal corporation may sue to enjoin an illegal act, involving the expenditure of funds raised by taxation, even, when it appears on the face of the complaint that the plaintiff's interest does not differ in kind from that of the public in general.

Taxpayers may question the legality of expenditures in Kentucky,[39] Ohio,[40] Wisconsin,[41] as well as in practically all the other states.

New York will allow the municipality as well as the taxpayer to question an expenditure of funds.[42] In Montana, the taxpayer has to wait until the money has actually been paid before suit can be brought,[43] but if it is alleged that the board members are insolvent, an injunction might issue to prevent payment. Illinois courts decided that a taxpayer might enjoin a board of education which sought to pay funds to a contract upon an alleged supplementary contract and compromise.[44] Taxpayers have been successful in maintaining suits to enjoin the use of money raised for building purposes from being used for other purposes.[45]

In Missouri the county clerk has to bring the suit, but, if he refuses to act, any freeholder may do so. In West Virginia the county superintendent may question the expenditures of the district boards and the state tax commission may question and enjoin a board from expending money in excess of revenue. Several other states give to the taxpayer the right to question expenditures, but, even in the absence of a statute, the common law upholds his right to question any expenditure upon the ground of legality, fraud, or capricious action on the part of the board.

Many cases might be cited to uphold the right of the citizen, taxpayer, or an interested party to enjoin expenditures planned to be made illegally. The point must be emphasized that it is only the legality of the action which may be questioned. Taxpayers

---

[38] Noble *v.* Davidson, 177 Ind. 19, 96 N. E. 325 (1911).

[39] Anderson *v.* Burton, Ky. App., 192 S. W. 519 (1917).

[40] Grant *v.* Brouse, 1 Ohio Nisi Prius 145 (1894).

[41] Milquet *v.* Van Straten, 186 Wis. 303, 202 N. W. 670 (1925).

[42] Warnock *v.* Wray, 194 N. Y. S. 396 (1922).

[43] State *ex rel.* Stephens *v.* Zuck, 67 Mont. 324, 215 P. 806 (1923).

[44] Board of Education *v.* Barracks, 235 Ill. App. 35 (1924).

[45] Miami Bank & Trust Co. *v.* Board of Education, 80 So. 307 (1918).

will not be successful in maintaining action when they seek to question the discretion of the board. When a board of education has the right to act, it may do so without interference, with the exceptions that their action is not tainted with fraud and is not capricious. The principle was discussed in greater detail under the heading of "Discretionary Powers of the Board."[46]

Attention is called to one type of statute which the records of the courts show to be a trouble maker. There is a great multiplicity of suits in the State of Oklahoma by taxpayers seeking to recover funds alleged to have been paid out illegally. An examination of the statutes suggests a reason for the trouble. One is a statute which makes board members individually liable for double the amount of the illegal expenditure and gives one-half of the sum recovered to the one who prosecutes the suit. The reports show that the real business of the schools has been interfered with on several occasions. Such a statute encourages an undue personal interest.

Personal Liability of Board Members and Officers of the Board for Acts Involved in the Administration of Expenditures

XII. Statutes imposing individual personal liability upon members of boards of education and their officers for unlawfully expending or disbursing money have been upheld rather strictly by the courts.

One of the principal means in force at the present time to secure honesty and strict adherence to statutory provisions is to make the board members and the officers who have any part in the transaction, or both, personally liable for the funds so unlawfully expended. This method has been a constant source of difficulty for the courts. The decision in the case of Sanborn *v.* Neal (1860) states the difficulties recognized at this early date.[47]

> In this case, as well as in all other cases, the intention of the parties governs, and, when a person known to be a public officer contracts with reference to public matters committed to his charge, he is presumed to act in his official capacity only, although the contract may not in terms allude to the character in which he acts, unless the officer by unmistakable language assumes a personal liability, or is guilty of fraud or misrepresentation. Being a public agent with his powers and duties prescribed by law, the extent of his powers are presumed to be as well known to all with whom he contracts as to himself.

[46] *Ante*, p. 16ff.

[47] Sanborn *v.* Neal, 4 Minn. 140, 77 Am. Dec. 502 (1860).

When, therefore, there is no want of good faith, a party contracts with such an officer with his eyes open, and has no one to blame if it should afterwards appear that the officer did not have the authority which it is supposed he had. Were the rule otherwise, few persons of responsibility would be found to serve the public in that large class of offices which require a sacrifice of time and perhaps money, but afford neither honor nor profit to the incumbent.

It should be pointed out at this time that this rule is different from the general rule applicable in private affairs where the agent is supposed to know his authority and he may be held personally if he fails to bind his principal.

The Sanborn case is widely cited and was upheld in 1918.[48]

Another case which also succinctly states the law and is widely quoted is that of Reed *v.* Conway [49] in which the court said:

From a careful examination of authorities from the case of Turner *v.* Sterling, 23 Car. II reported in 2 Ventris 26, down to . . . our own times, both in English and American courts, the doctrine that a ministerial officer, acting in a matter before him with discretionary power, or acting in a matter before him judicially, or as a quasi-judge is not responsible to any one receiving an injury from such act, unless the officer act maliciously and willfully wrong, is most clearly established and maintained.

An extremely hard fought case,[50] concerned the personal liability of board members for loss due to the fact that the wrong form of bond was accepted by the board of education through mistake and ignorance. The surety company furnishing the bond for the contractor and acting as his guarantor made the bond out on a form used for private individuals instead of a form applying to public corporations. The courts held the board responsible in both suits. In 1924, however, another case [51] overruled the Burton case on the ground that, when a surety bond is given to a school board, the court should read into it the state statute on the subject matter thereof. These cases seem to indicate a responsibility on the part of the state to furnish to school boards the correct statutory form of bond, so that lawsuits of this type would be avoided and public money and property be properly protected. It certainly does not seem reasonable that a board of education be held personally responsible for such a legal technicality. This

[48] Hendrix *v.* Morris, Ark. 203 S. W. 1008.

[49] Reed *v.* Conway, 20 Mo. 22 (1854).

[50] Burton Machinery Co. *v.* Ruth *et al.*, Mo. 186 S. W. 737 (1916); Burton Machinery Co. *v.* Ruth *et al.*, Mo. 194 S. W. 526 (1917).

[51] Fogarty *v.* Davis, 305 Mo. 288, 264 S. W. 879 (1924).

emphasizes again the principle being followed in other parts of this study, that the state must assume responsibility and guide boards of education in technical matters, especially those which arise but infrequently in a board's affairs.

The theory that public officials should be personally liable for their acts in the administration of expenditures is fundamental in the English law:

> The theory of the English Law, as previously pointed out, is that any official who in the discharge of his public functions does anything for which he has not lawful authority, is in respect of that particular action to be treated as an ordinary private citizen . . . however much he may have believed himself to be fulfilling his duty, either in obedience to orders or upon his own responsibility . . . and is therefore liable in the ordinary courts. In the civil courts an action for damages may be brought against him; or alternatively he may be prosecuted in the criminal courts.[52]

The Statutes and Personal Responsibility

In order to make the members of the board of education or any of their officers personally liable for acts done in the line of their duty, there must be a statutory enactment defining the responsibility. Board of Education members have been held responsible for co-mingling funds and using up the "teachers' fund" for building purposes in view of a statute covering such matters,[53] and members have been held responsible even though they did not vote for a contract made in violation of the law. These board members were present at a meeting when a contract was let without submitting to bids, and, although not voting for the contract, they voiced no objection to it.[54]

Board members have also been held responsible for misapplying funds,[55] expending money without warrant of law,[56] exceeding estimate as appropriated,[57] and where they clearly acted as individuals.[58]

A board member cannot escape individual responsibility by resigning.[59]

[52] Ashley, Percy, *Local and Central Government*, p. 369.
[53] Consolidated School District No. 6 *v.* Shawhan, Ky. 273, S. W. 182 (1925).
[54] Audit Hanover Township School District, Pa. 108 A. 656 (1919).
[55] Powell *v.* Mathews, County Superintendent, Texas Civ. App. 280 S. W. 903 (1926).
[56] Douglas *v.* Talbot, 93 W. Va. 618, 117 S. E. 478 (1923).
[57] Lacey *v.* Board of Education, 98 Okla. 237, 224 P. 712 (1924).
[58] State Bank Reeseville *v.* Krenberger, 140 Wis. 517, 122 N. W. 1132 (1909).
[59] School District No. 2 *v.* Richards, 62 Mont. 319, 205 P. 206 (1922).

Treasurer's Personal Liability for Acts Done with Reference to the Expenditure and Disbursement of Money

It is axiomatic that the treasurer of a school district should be held personally responsible for embezzlement or conversion of funds. His personal responsibility for loss of funds through failure of the depository, loss of funds in transit, etc. is not so clear. However, some interesting questions arise as to his responsibility for administration of expenditures, which is a quite different responsibility from that involved in the care and custody of funds in the situations mentioned above.

In the first place, the treasurer has been held responsible for and personally liable for the payment of funds in case the warrant is not in the proper form,[60] for refusal to pay out upon proper order money in hand,[61] and for diverting money from one fund to another.[62]

In Arkansas [63] a rather peculiar case is reported. The board members were held not responsible for ordering the payment of money for illegal purposes, but the poor treasurer was held responsible for paying out the funds. Let the Court tell how it arrived at such a conclusion.

> A different rule, however, applies to the treasurer. He is only authorized to pay out money on orders or warrants of the board of directors of the school district when "properly drawn." The law requires that the directors shall draw orders on the treasurer for payment of wages or for any other lawful purpose, . . . When a warrant therefore is presented to the treasurer for payment for an unauthorized purpose, the treasurer pays the same at his own peril, and is personally and individually liable for the moneys unlawfully expended.

It seems rather remarkable reasoning which would place the onus upon a lone treasurer acting presumably on facts which were in regular order. Such reasoning would place judicial responsibility upon the treasurer and, if he were to question the legality of every expenditure, an unintended control would be placed over finances. The purpose of the discussion is to show how penalties and poorly written laws will sometimes place controls where we do not expect to find them. It is true that the treasurer has cer-

---

[60] School District *v.* Correll, 22 P. Mo. 322, 286 S. W. 136 (1926).
[61] Edson *v.* Hayden, 18 Wis. 657 (1864).
[62] School District No. 5 *v.* Long, Mich. 165 N. W. 604 (1917).
[63] Hendrix *v.* Morris, Ark., 203 S. W. 1008 (1918).

tain duties with reference to the care and custody of funds which should be strictly interpreted, but why he should be charged with discretion over the acts of the board of education, or personal responsibility for carrying out their orders seems to be beyond reason.

It would seem that a treasurer would not pay out money except upon the presentation of an order, but a Minnesota court found it necessary to hold a treasurer responsible for paying out funds without a warrant, order, or voucher being presented.[64]

The right of a treasurer to hold intact a fund amounting to $10,000, when vouchers had been duly issued for two-thirds of this amount, upon the personal request of the President of the Board of Education for the purpose of repaying a loan, was denied.[65] The immediate cause for the controversy getting into the courts was the fact that the bank in which the money was deposited failed in the meantime.

What Are the Penalties Which Most Surely Will Insure Compliance with the Law?

The determination of the penalties which should be exacted from members of a board of education when acting either as individuals or as official bodies is a very difficult matter to decide. This study makes no final attempt to solve this problem. This code, however, has been developed on the theory that if all the actions of the board are definitely defined, and the board is given all the power it should be allowed to exercise; and, furthermore, that if there are a sufficient number of checks, the number of acts requiring severe penalties will be reduced.

Penalties have been classed as:

1. Retributive
2. Deterrent
3. Preventive
4. Reformatory
5. Educative [66]

Emphasis in the proposed code has been placed upon the preventive and educative methods of imposing penalties. The retributive and deterrent forms are to be used only when the former do not work.

---

[64] First National Bank Duluth *v.* School District No. 15, Carlton 173, Minn. 383, 217 N. W. 366 (1928). [65] Reed *v.* People, 34 Wyo. 189, 242 P. 319 (1926).

[66] Willoughby, W. W., *Rational Basis for Legal Institutions*, p. 555.

The proposed code proposes to place the power of removal in the hands of the State Commissioner of Education. In case money has been fraudulently and wilfully converted to the use of officials or their friends, there is a reimbursement of the damage done and also the possibility of criminal prosecution.[67]

---

[67] Proposed Code, Art. VIII, sec. 14.

CHAPTER IX

SUMMARY AND CONCLUSIONS

Any problem of financial administration must be viewed from two standpoints, the legal or political, and the technical or service. This study is concerned primarily with the legal aspects of the control of expenditures of the public schools. It is impossible, however, to separate the legal from the technical as they are so closely interwoven and dependent upon each other. Before any defensible legal control should be set up, it is necessary to know the nature and types of technical or service systems which are likely to be in operation. The law can, of course, modify the service systems, but it is also true that the people in control of the actual organization and management can also modify the practical application of the law. Laws will not enforce themselves, and it is especially hard to enforce laws which are not whole-heartedly supported by the people whose duty it is to carry them out.

It has not been this investigator's problem to create or suggest new types of accounting systems, forms of procedure for the payment of warrants, or any of the other multifarious service jobs connected with the administration of expenditures. Reliance has been placed upon the investigations of others in these fields and the opinions of authorities. The legal control as proposed in this code suggested is an attempt to suggest means whereby the results of these researches, and the principles advocated by the recognized authorities may be effectively put into operation.

The problem of devising the legal controls which will properly regulate, apportion, and secure the enforcement of the powers of control led to some considerations of fundamental questions of political science.

The more important of these problems considered in this study were:

I. The legal relation of the state and the local school district.

II. The relative advantages of administrative and legislative control.

III. The separation of powers of control as between the state administrative agencies and those of the local school districts.

IV. The safeguards which must be established in granting powers to administrative bodies.

V. The legal relation of the city government to the local board of education.

VI. The nature and extent of state control which should follow grants of aid to local school districts.

VII. The nature and extent of the supervision which should be exercised by the state board of education over the local boards of education.

VIII. The relation of the legislative to the executive officials in all divisions of the school organization.

IX. The type of technical or service organizations which will be most likely to work under our conceptions of democratic ideals.

Conclusions with Reference to These Problems

I. The legal relation of the state to the local school district is fixed by law. The courts uphold the constitutional and statutory provisions establishing the fact that the schools are state institutions. This status has not been questioned by educational authorities.

II. The legislatures have been attempting to regulate and direct by statutory law many details of school administration for which there are no definite standards and no accepted theory warranting such regulations.

All matters of control should first be considered from the standpoint of whether or not the matter can better be regulated by statute or left to administrative determination.

This study follows the criteria established by Freund which direct that matters be left to administrative control:

1. When it is difficult to separate the lawful from the unlawful.
2. When no definite standards are available.
3. When it is necessary or desirable to check compliance with the legal enactments.
4. When liberty and initiative are desired.[1]

This study supports the proposition that, under these criteria, the regulation of school expenditures should be largely a matter of

[1] See *ante*, pp. 25ff.

administrative control. The proposed code is largely concerned with the methods of control and the setting up of safeguards for the control of the administration. The definite objectives are to provide the greatest flexibility of organization and administration, and, at the same time, definitely to place an absolute power of control over the administrative bodies or their officers when they fail to act in accordance with the legislative principles established.

III. The separation of the powers as between the state administrative body and that of the local district is still a vexatious problem. The principal problems are those concerned with the setting up of checks and balances which will insure coöperation between the two bodies and keep to a minimum autocratic and mechanical state control. It is desired that the state make available the expert advice, the best experience, and vision of those who are so situated as to see the problems of administration in larger relief. The proposed code gives to the state board of education more power than is now given in most of the states, but it is to be noted that such power is checked as to the manner and form of action, which checks are definitely intended to produce the coöperation and feeling of mutual confidence which is desired.

IV. In granting powers of control to administrative bodies or officials, certain safeguards should be set up. These safeguards should be established over every governmental body and official to whom discretionary authority is granted. Following Carr's criteria [2] effective means of accomplishing these purposes are:

1. Delegation of authority only to a trustworthy body which can command confidence.
2. The limits of delegated power must be definitely laid down.
3. Interested advice must be welcomed and taken into consideration.
4. The public must have notice of the regulations of the administrative body.
5. There must be machinery for quick revocation of authority or amendment thereto.

V. The nature and extent of control which should follow grants of aid must be of such a nature that it will accomplish the purposes intended when such aid is granted, and yet must not hinder the development of initiative and liberty of action on the part of the body to which it is given. The recognition of the safeguards enumerated above will in most instances accomplish this end.

[2] See *ante*, pp. 39ff.

VI. Supervision may become more burdensome than absolute direction. The principle so well established in law that the schools are state institutions commits the state to a supervisory policy. The principal problem is to exercise this supervision in such a way as to secure coöperation, mutual respect, and confidence as between the state and the local school district.

VII. There should be a clearcut distinction between the legislative functions of the policy-making bodies such as the state and local boards of education and their executive officers.

VIII and IX. The service divisions must be viewed from the standpoint of the nature of our political system. The systems of purchasing, contracting, accounting, auditing, and reporting are but means to secure efficiency and honesty of administration. The methods and means of accomplishing these aims may be varied. It is therefore unwise to stifle the initiative of local units by inflexible regulations. Such regulation, supervision, and inspection must be of such a nature as to enable the people, the state and the school officials, themselves, to see and understand the operations of their administrative unit. It is therefore necessary that a uniform system up to a certain point is desirable, but there must always be a way left open for the exercise of initiative and liberty of action by those who actually have the responsibility of carrying the policies into effect.

This study of the administrative law regulating school expenditures has revealed a paucity of legal research in the fields of the relations between administrative bodies and officers engaged in the administration of education. The only studies which have been made have come from within the ranks of those engaged in school administration. There are numerous studies made from the standpoint of the national and state administrative officers, but few of these touch the problems of school administration.

The research needed is not primarily to find the rules of law, but to discover the principles and theories which cause the courts to decide the cases coming before them as they do. It is this latter type of study that has not been done for the field of education. Students of administrative law in the law schools are concerned principally in the organization and powers of such administrative bodies and officers as the Inter-State Commerce Commission, the Income Tax Division of the Treasury, the Public Utilities Commissions, and bodies of like nature. The problems of school administration are in many respects different from other governmental problems. For example, the schools are conducted by professionally trained and appointed officers; while other administrative officers may be appointed, such officials are, for the most part, untrained. Should such professionally trained people be controlled in the same manner as those who have but a short tenure, subject directly to political control and lacking a professional training? Students of education with a background of political theory and possessing a knowledge of how to study law should be encouraged to undertake research in this field of law. If the work is to be done in the immediate future, the experience of the past would indicate that such research will have to be done by the students from within the field of educational administration.

With reference to the technical or service divisions, particularly those relating to the practical problems of form, organization, and methods of procedure, it is the conclusion of this investigator that these matters can be better regulated by administrative action than by statutory laws. The legislature will have extremely important problems to solve in setting up the statutory regulations which will properly control the administration. If the legislature is able to formulate and enact a law which will produce a high-grade accounting system, it is performing a high-grade service to the people. It would appear that such a duty well performed requires a higher grade of constructive statesmanship than the enactment of the details of an accounting system which may at the time of enactment represent the best thought but may be obsolete shortly after being put into operation. Control of this type of a matter is surely a legislative function, but this power must be so exercised as to provide for the flexibility and initiative necessary in our complex society. The legislature must delegate the regulation of many details to the administrative bodies. This study has attempted to suggest methods and types of administrative organization which will produce desirable results.

The conclusions reached with reference to the details of legal control as established by the courts and legislatures will not be repeated in this concluding chapter. The summary at the beginning of each chapter enumerates the specific conclusions reached after a careful study of the law and the authorities. An enumeration of these detailed conclusions would not serve any useful purpose by their repetition here, without the supporting evidence.

The proposed provisions of a code for the regulation of expenditures is an important outcome of this research. It represents a proposal of statutory provisions which will establish by law and provide for the machinery to put into effect the most defensible types and systems of organization and control of school expenditures which this investigator has been able to find and evaluate.

It is hoped that this research pointing out these general principles of organization and control of the administration may be elaborated upon, further studied and tested, and applied to other fields of school administration.

APPENDIX A

PROPOSED CODE PROVISIONS[1]

An Act to establish, organize, and provide for the support of a system of free public schools for the State of ———. Be it enacted by the people of the State of———:

ARTICLE I. SHORT TITLE.

This Act shall be known as
the "Education Law."

ARTICLE II. EDUCATION LAW TO BE LIBERALLY CONSTRUED.

The rule of the common law
that statutes in derogation thereof
are to be strictly construed,
has no application in this Education Law.
The Education Law
establishes the law of this State
respecting the subjects
to which it relates and its provisions,
and all proceedings under it
are to be liberally construed,
with a view to effect its objects
and to promote justice.[2]

ARTICLE III. DEFINITION OF TERMS.

As used in this act
the following specified terms
mean as here defined.

1. Board of Education.

The term "board of education" shall
include by whatever name known
the governing body
charged with the general control,
management, and responsibility
of the schools of any city,
county, or school district.

---

[1] The proposals are made for the legal control of the financial administration of school districts. These proposals are suggested as an integral part of the general education law of any state. It should be remembered in inspecting this code that the proposals are made primarily for the regulation of expenditures.

These provisions will fit in with those of any general school code. Such divisions of this code as Articles I, II, and III, which would be integral parts of any general school code, are but incidental parts of this study.

[2] Adapted from Political Code, California, sec. 4.

2. Superintendent.

The term "superintendent" shall mean the chief executive officer of a school district.

3. School Officials.

The term "school officials" shall include clerk, secretary, treasurer, trustee or member of the board of education, superintendent of schools, business manager, or any other elective or appointive officer of a school district.

4. This Act.

Whenever the words, "this act" are used herein they shall refer to the entire Education Law, as herein enacted.

5. Public Notice.

Whenever the term "public notice" is used in this act it shall be defined as follows: Publication of a notice stating the purpose and objects of the event to which the public is entitled to notice, published in a daily newspaper for at least three issues, the first publication being made at least two weeks in advance of the event for which public notice is being given.

Provided, in case no daily newspaper is published within the school district, two consecutive insertions in a weekly newspaper published during the two weeks prior to the event so advertised, or in case no newspaper is published within the school district, then publication in any newspaper of general circulation in the district shall be deemed sufficient notice.

6. Public Hearing.

The words "public hearing" as used in this act shall mean a public meeting held in a conveniently located auditorium, under the regular rules and regulations of the board of education, to which any adult resident of the school district shall be welcomed and in which meeting he shall be encouraged to participate.

Provided, the persons present may
by resolution determine the procedure
and fix the conditions under
which persons present may be heard.
The president of the board of education
or someone designated by him
shall be the presiding officer of the meeting.

ARTICLE IV. THE STATE BOARD OF EDUCATION.

Section 1. General Powers of State Board of Education.

The State Board of Education
shall exercise
through the State Commissioner of Education,
and his professional assistants,
general control and supervision
over the public schools
and all other educational institutions
of the State of ———.

Section 2. Specific Powers of State Board of Education.[3]

The State Board of Education
shall have power to establish and
enforce through the State Commissioner of Education,
such minimum regulations and standards
with reference to each of the following matters,
as it may determine
to be reasonable and just:

a. Buildings and sites.
b. Salaries to be paid to teachers and school officials of the State.
c. The type and curricula of each and every type of special school, and the conditions under which each type of school or class may be established.
d. Purposes for which public funds may be expended.
e. Textbooks, maps, charts, equipment, and supplies of each and every description.
f. Accounting systems for each type of school district.
g. Uniform budget system and procedure for each type of school district.
h. Uniform records and reports for each type of school district.
i. Audit of accounts and of the values received for funds expended.
j. Care and custody of school funds.
k. Transportation of pupils.
l. Closing of the fiscal year.

Section 3. Delegation of Power to Control State Aid Policies.

The State Board of Education shall in accordance
with the general plan
and principles

[3] It must also be noted that these somewhat detailed sections of the powers of the State Board of Education relate only to such features of the organization as are necessary to control expenditures properly. A comprehensive code, delegating control and power over other school matters to the State Board of Education, would have to be detailed in the same manner as these sections were developed.

established by the legislature,
apportion, distribute, and administer
all state school funds
and require that its use
shall accomplish
the purposes for
which it was designed.

Section 4. Provision for Interested Advice and Coöperation.

It is the desire and command
of the legislature
that the powers granted to
the State Board of Education
be determined by the State Board of Education
and executed by the State Commissioner of Education
in accordance
with the spirit of
democratic institutions.

Therefore, before any general administrative code,
regulation, or rule
be adopted or promulgated,
by the State Board of Education,
that the educational leaders of the State,
such as superintendents of schools,
teachers, and principals of schools,
representatives of boards of education,
members of faculties of state institutions, and interested citizens
may have opportunity,
after reasonable notice,
in a personal or group conference
to make available
such knowledge, advice, or research
which any of these interested persons
mentioned may possess.

Furthermore, that before the
adoption or promulgation
of any type of regulation or rule
affecting any particular type of school organization
that representatives of such schools and other educational leaders
may have opportunity to make available
their knowledge and opinions in the same manner
as directed for the
establishment of general codes or regulations.

Section 5. Legislative Power to Revoke or Restrict Powers Granted.

The Legislature shall retain power
to allow or to deny,
to extend or to limit or
modify in any way,
at any time,
the powers of the
State Board of Education, or
the State Commissioner of Education.

Section 6. Power of State Board to Enforce its Commands.

The State Board of Education
shall have power to enforce its
established codes, regulations, and orders
by removing from office any member
of a board of education,
the superintendent of schools
or any other officer or employee
of the local district who
by any act of omission or commission
wilfully fails to obey
any such mandate of the
State Board of Education.

Provided, that in case any
act of commission or omission
on the part of any member or members of a board of education,
the superintendent of schools or any other employee,
should result in pecuniary loss to the school district
the State Board of Education through the
State Commissioner of Education
shall institute action in
the courts for the recovery
of such funds from those
who are legally responsible for the loss, and
such sums recovered shall be placed to the
credit of the school district.

ARTICLE V. THE STATE COMMISSIONER OF EDUCATION.

Section 1. Powers of the State Commissioner of Education.

The State Commissioner of Education
is hereby charged with
the following powers and duties:[4]

1. He is the executive officer
of the State Board of Education.

2. He shall enforce all
general or special laws relating to the
educational system of the state.

3. He shall execute
all educational policies
as determined by
the State Board of Education.[5]

4. He shall have general supervision
over all the schools of the state.

---

[4] Only those powers of a general nature which are applicable and necessary to control expenditures are enumerated. Many other desirable regulations and powers concerning other phases of school work would be included in a general school code. All such delegated powers in order to be held constitutional must be definitely and specifically enumerated.

[5] Adapted from New York Education Law, sec. 94, which has been upheld in the courts of that State.

5. He shall publish, promulgate, and enforce standards, regulations, rules, and codes established by the State Board of Education concerning the matters enumerated under Article IV. of this act.

6. He shall have power to act for and in the name of the State Board of Education and he shall have power to enforce his own or the rulings of the State Board of Education, upon his own volition, or by action in any court of law.

Section 2. Appeals to State Commissioner of Education.

Any person conceiving himself aggrieved may appeal or petition to the Commissioner of Education, who is hereby authorized and required to examine and decide the same; and the Commissioner of Education may also institute such proceedings as are authorized under this act and his decision in such appeals, petitions, or proceedings shall be final and conclusive, and not subject to review in any place or court whatever. Such appeal or petition may be made in consequence of any action,[6] or failure to act:

1. By any school district meeting;
2. By the board of education or any school official relating to any matter concerning the

a. preparation, adoption, interpretation, or administration of the annual school budget or
b. what purports to be an expenditure for public education, the
c. accounting system,
d. audit,
e. the publicity given to any fiscal matter,
f. the duties of any official concerned with the administration of school moneys, or
g. the form and legality of any contract, or
h. specifications for contracts,
i. award of contracts, or
j. transportation of pupils.

---

[6] This paragraph of the code to this point is quoted verbatim from the New York Education Law, Art. 34, sec. 891.

This law confers the broadest powers of appeal of any State in the United States, and has been upheld repeatedly in the courts.

Section 3. Powers of Commissioner Upon Appeals or Petitions.

The Commissioner of Education,
in reference to such appeals, petitions, or proceedings,
shall have power:

1. To regulate practice therein.
2. To determine whether an appeal
shall stay proceedings,
and prescribe conditions upon which,
it shall or
shall not operate.[7]

Section 4. Power to Hold Inquiry.

The State Commissioner of Education,
or some official of the Department of Education,
whom he shall designate,
shall have power to conduct an inquiry
concerning any matter subject to regulation
by the State Board of Education.

Provided, such inquiry shall be conducted in the local
school district, in accordance with rules and procedure
established by the State Board of Education,
and that the person conducting the inquiry
shall have power to summon and compel
the presence of witnesses and
take testimony under oath.

ARTICLE VI. PREPARATION AND ADOPTION OF THE BUDGET.

Section 1. Estimate of Revenues and Expenses—Tentative Budget.[8]

The superintendent of each school district in the State of ———
shall be and act as budget officer of such district.
He shall, as such budget officer,
prepare and file
with the board of education of such district,
on or before June 1 of each year,
a tentative budget,
which shall set forth in detail
the estimated revenues
and proposed expenditures
for the ensuing fiscal year.

This tentative budget shall be made available at once,
and placed on file with the secretary of the board
for public inspection
and copies shall be furnished without cost
to any elector of the district
and shall continue so available
for at least fifteen days prior
to the public hearing upon the budget
as hereinafter provided.

---

[7] Quoted directly from New York Education Law, Art. 34, sec. 891.

[8] Details as to what should go into this tentative budget are not enumerated in the code, as these details definitely are matters which should be left to administrative regulation by the state department of public instruction.

Section 2. Notice and Hearing.

Fifteen days
after the submission of the tentative budget to the board of education
by the budget officer,
the board of education
shall hold a public hearing
for the purpose of considering
the tentative budget for the next fiscal year as
presented by the budget officer.

Provided, that public notice of the
public hearing, as defined in this act
shall have been given.

Section 3. Adoption of Budget.

At the close of the public hearing or
within ten days thereafter,
the board of education shall meet
and adopt the budget as
presented by the budget officer,
or with such changes as seem necessary and desirable
as determined by the board,
upon a majority vote of the board
by a yea and nay vote
upon each item so changed.

Section 4. Appropriation of Funds.

The adoption of the budget
as presented or as amended
shall be deemed and is an appropriation
of the fund or funds
for the purposes
stated in the
expenditure budget.

Section 5. Expenditures Must Not Exceed Income or Appropriations Made.

It shall be unlawful
for any board of education
to make any appropriations
or expend or
contract to expend any money
in excess of
the estimated expendable income
for the fiscal year
included in the budget.

Section 6. Failure to Adopt Budget.

In case any board of education should fail
to adopt a budget,
on or before July 1 as
provided in this act
for any cause or reason,
the last legal budget adopted
shall be deemed to be adopted

and appropriations made in accordance therewith,
until such time as the board
shall regularly adopt a budget.

Section 7. Budget and Expenditures.

Except as hereinafter provided,
the expenditures program as adopted in the
budget and appropriation plan,
must be followed
by the board of education and its executive officers.

Section 8. No Expenditure Without Appropriation.

It shall be unlawful
for any board of education
to authorize, allow,
or contract for the expenditure of money,
unless it has been appropriated
as provided for in this act.
Any contract made in violation
of any provision of this act
shall be null and void.

Section 9. Transfers.

The board of education of any school district
shall have the power to authorize
the transfer of
any current, unencumbered balance
from any appropriation division to another division;
Provided notice of such proposed change
is published and public hearing held
in the same manner as the
notice and hearing is provided for
in the adoption of the original budget plan.

Transfers between any items
of the same division of the
expenditure budget
may be authorized
at any regular meeting
of the board of education.

All votes upon changes in
the appropriations of expenditures
shall be by a majority vote
of the members of the board
upon a recorded *yea* and *nay* vote.

Section 10. Emergencies.

The board of education of any school district,
in the event of emergencies,
which involve unusual expenditures not provided for
by the expenditure budget,
is hereby authorized to appropriate
and expend funds in excess of estimated income,
to cover the cost of such additional expenditures
made necessary by such emergency.

Provided, an emergency as herein defined shall consist of
expenditures made necessary because of
unusual and exceptional
increase in population or
sudden and unforeseen changes in the
purchasing power of money,
floods, fires, epidemics, or
other causes generally classed
as Acts of God or
the public enemy.

Provided further,
such authorization shall be passed
at a regular or special meeting of the board of education,
after such notice and hearing
has been given as provided for
the adoption of the original budget.

Provided further, the amount of such
additional expenditures
or such part as the board may direct
shall be included as a special and specific appropriation
in the next budget to be adopted.

Provided further, that no financial
contingency shall ever warrant the
closing of any school, except
with the permission of the
State Board of Education.
In case such a contingency seems imminent
the State Board of Education may,
rather than to authorize the closing of the schools,
take charge of the schools
of such district until such
time as the financial affairs may be
placed upon a sound foundation.

Section 11. Encumbrances Upon Appropriations.

Any contract made,
requisition issued, or order placed,
by any board of education
or its duly authorized agent,
for goods to be delivered,
or services to be rendered,
shall constitute from the date of the issue and
to the extent of the
full amount of such
contract, order, or requisition
an encumbrance against the funds
apportioned for purposes
represented by such contract, order, or requisition.

Section 12. Fiscal Year.

The fiscal year
of each and every school district
shall commence on the first day of July annually,
and close on the last day of June following.

Provided, that the State Board of Education
shall make such regulations
as it may deem proper and necessary
in closing the fiscal year of all school districts,
so as to insure the payment of all just claims,
which are outstanding and unpaid
and which are just charges
against the revenue of the fiscal year in which contracted.

Section 13. Borrowing Money for Current Expenses.

Each board of education
shall have power,
by regularly adopted resolution,
when obligations are due and
it does not have available funds
with which to pay them,
to borrow money and
issue notes therefore and
pledge the anticipated current
revenues of the
school district
for the payment of the same.

Provided, the total sum so borrowed,
shall not at any one time,
exceed the unpledged total amount
estimated to be received
from all sources and
available for use
during the current fiscal year
in which such money is borrowed.

Provided further,
that every resolution
authorizing the borrowing of money
shall contain a statement of the
unpledged estimated income
available for the fiscal year
in which the money is borrowed.

Provided further,
that the maturity of any
note or other evidence of indebtedness
shall not fall later
than the date closing the fiscal year
during which such money is borrowed.

Section 14. Surplus Funds.

Any school district
having a surplus of funds available
after the payment of all claims
against the current funds
of any fiscal year have been paid,
may make either of the following
dispositions of such surplus:

First, retirement of outstanding bonds of the school district, or
secondly, apply the same toward the
reduction of local taxation
for the ensuing fiscal year.

Section 15. Penalties.

Any member of a board of education
or any administrative officer
found guilty of wilfully violating
any provision of this act,
may be removed from office,
after notice and hearing,
by the State Commissioner of Education.

Provided,
that in the event the school district is made
to suffer any pecuniary loss or damage,
due to any act of commission or omission,
of any member or members of the board
or any officers of the board,
as enumerated in any part of this Article VI
of this act,
each member or officer shall be individually
liable to the extent of such loss to the school district.
Such penalty and loss may be recovered
upon motion of any resident taxpayer
before a court of law or
in action taken by the State Commissioner of Education.

ARTICLE VII.

Section 1. Tax Levy.

The board of education of each school district shall,
on or before the first day of July of each year,[9]
and is hereby empowered to levy
upon all of the property located within such school district,
and subject to taxation,
a tax sufficient to raise the amount of money
estimated in the income budget
as necessary to be raised by local taxation
to pay all current and continuing obligations
of the district for the ensuing fiscal year.

The secretary of the board
shall certify and deliver at once
the resolution of the board
to the ——————————[10]
which (who) shall place and include

[9] This date presumes that the fiscal affairs of the governmental units run from July to July. The date may be changed to fit the local needs and customs.

[10] Insert here the name of the person, body, or bodies which makes up the tax duplicate and authorizes and collects the taxes. It is the plan to adapt this code to present governmental machinery for the care of the ministerial acts necessary to combine this levy with others and to provide for the collection of the same. This may be the city council, board of supervisors, fiscal court, or other body charged by law with this administrative duty.

such levy upon the tax rolls
and authorize the collection of the same
as all other taxes are imposed and collected.

Provided, that no tax levy shall be
in excess of the
constitutional or
statutory limitations.

Section 2. Emergencies.

The board of education in each school district
is hereby authorized to levy
in the same manner as current taxes are levied,
a tax which will raise
such amounts as the board may direct
to pay in whole or in part
the debts created because of emergencies,
as provided in Article VI, Section 10 of this act.

ARTICLE VIII. EXECUTION OF THE EXPENDITURE BUDGET.

Section 1. General Powers Granted to the Board of Education.

The board of education of
each and every school district
is hereby vested with all the power necessary
to properly administer the financial affairs
of the schools under its jurisdiction.

Section 2. Power of Board to Determine Purposes and Policies.

The board of education of
each and every school district
shall have the power
tó determine
each and all of the purposes
and policies for which
money is to be expended.

Section 3. Delegation of Authority.

The board of education of
each and every school district
shall have the power to
delegate the execution of the
expenditure budget
to the superintendent of schools
or to his assistant in charge of business affairs,
under such rules and regulations
as the board of education
may establish.

Section 4. Approval of Contracts.

Subdivision *a*.

All contracts, orders, or requisitions
made by the executive officers of the board
shall be approved at the first regular meeting
of the board of education following
the consummation of such contracts.

Subdivision *b*.

Approval by the board of education
of the contract
shall be considered and deemed
approval of the order to
pay the claim made under the terms of such contract,
when regularly certified and attested and
all other formalities are
complied with as provided in this act.

Subdivision *c*.

In the case the board of education
should fail to approve any contract
made by its executive officers, the
status quo of the board and the parties
with whom the executive officers are
dealing shall be as if no
contract had ever been agreed upon.

Subdivision *d*.

Provided, should any goods have been
delivered and used, or
any services have been rendered
to the benefit of the board of education,
such sum shall be paid by the board
to the parties upon *quantum meruit*
but no damages shall be assessed
as against the board of education
for failure to consummate the agreement
made by the executive officers.

Subdivision *e*.

Provided, further, that no liability
whatsoever shall attach to the board of education
in case the executive officers act beyond
the authority definitely delegated to
such officer by the board.

Section 5. Contracts Must Be in Writing.

All contracts made by a board of education or its
executive officers which require
expenditures of funds in
excess of $50.00 must be reduced
to a writing and signed by the contracting parties or
their authorized agents.

Section 6. Contracts In Excess of $250 Must Be Let After Notice and Bids.

Subdivision *a*.

All contracts,
other than those for personal service,
and the textbooks
which involve expenditures
during any fiscal year of sums
exceeding $250.00

shall be made only
after public notice to
parties who may be interested
in making proposals under such
conditions as the board of education
may propose.

Subdivision *b*.

Provided, before public notice
is given as provided in this act,
that full and complete specifications, plans,
proposal forms, and
conditions of award and delivery,
shall be prepared and copies
furnished upon demand to
any prospective bidder.

Provided, further, that it shall be unlawful
for any board of education
to change or modify in any important detail
conditions, specifications, proposal, or plan,
after the award of the contract.

Subdivision *c*.

The board of education
shall let all contracts
to the lowest responsible bidder,
quality and service being considered.

Provided, that the board of education
shall have power to reject all proposals
and readvertise for new proposals.

Subdivision *d*.

The board of education shall have power
in cases of emergency,
such as immediate and necessary
repairs to boilers,
plumbing systems, and small
partial losses caused by
fires or floods,
to contract to have such
work done without
the formality of
public notice and letting.

Section 7. Certification of Appropriation.

Each and every contract entered into
by a board of education
involving an expenditure
greater than $50.00
shall have a certificate attached,
signed by the superintendent of schools
or his assistant in charge of business affairs,
certifying that the amount of money necessary to meet

the contract price
has been lawfully appropriated in the expenditure budget
for such purpose.

Provided, further, that there is
certification by the same officials that
there is money in the treasury,
or in the process of collection,
to the credit of the appropriate fund
free from any previous encumbrance.

Provided, further, that the certification and contract
shall constitute an encumbrance
upon such fund until paid or lawfully rescinded.

Section 8. Prohibition of Pecuniary Interest in Contracts.

No board of education
nor any school official
shall make any contract
with any of its own members
or with any firm or corporation in which
any member or official of the board
shall be directly or indirectly interested.

Provided that contracts for
personal service shall not be made
with relatives of any board member or school official,
if such relative is within the second degree of
consanguinity.

Provided, that in rural areas,
if after advertising
for proposals for transportation of pupils
has been made and no responsible and reasonable
proposals are made, such a board
of education may, with the consent
of the State Commissioner of Education,
enter into a contract for such transportation,
with their own members or in which he
may be pecuniarily interested.

Provided, further, that officials
may contract for their own services
with the board of education, or to
furnish their own transportation in the
necessary conduct of the duties of their office.

Section 9. Contracts Made in Violation of Act Are Null and Void.

Any contract made in
violation of any provision
of this article
shall be null and void.

Section 10. Publicity.

Each and every board of education
shall at least once each year
make a full and complete

report of the expenditures for the
last fiscal year
to the citizens of the school district,
either by publishing the same in a newspaper
of general circulation or
publishing the same in pamphlet form.

Section 11. Books Must Be Open to the Public.

Each and every board of education
shall allow, during business hours,
a full inspection of its books and financial records
by any interested citizen.

Section 12. Expenditures May Be Made Outside School District.

Each and every board of education
shall have power to expend the funds of the
school district,
for services rendered to it
outside the school district,
and shall also have power to coöperate
with other school districts
in maintaining any type of
educational service or organization
which it may deem
to be to the best interests of the schools
of the district.

Section 13. Yea and Nay Vote Upon Expenditure of Funds.

All motions
involving the expenditure of money
must be passed by an affirmative vote
of the board upon a recorded
yea and nay vote
of the quorum present.

Section 14. Penalties.

Subdivision *a*.

Any member of a board of education
or any official who
wilfully, maliciously, fraudulently, or collusively,
agrees to or does not voice a protest
against acts in violation of
any of the provisions of this article of this act,
shall be removed from office by
the State Commissioner of Education
in accordance with procedure
determined by that State Department of Education.

Provided, that if any court of law
shall determine that any board member or
official of the board shall be guilty
of fraud, collusion, or personal profit
from any transaction of the board, shall
be fined the amount of the loss to

the board of education, but in no case less than $10.00
or in the discretion of the court may be
sentenced to imprisonment in the
state penitentiary for a
period of not less than one year
nor more than five years.

Provided, further, that all fines,
shall be paid to the
school district suffering loss.

APPENDIX B

CHECK LIST FOR LEGAL TOPICS BEARING UPON THE CONTROL OF EXPENDITURES

The following list of legal topics was used for tracing possible decisions bearing upon the problem of determining the legal rights and responsibilities of boards of education and school officials in the administration of the expenditure program. The source of the classification of topics is the Index to the First and Second Decennial Digests, West Publishing Company, St. Paul.

General and Sub-Headings in American Digest System

Schools and School Districts:	Key Number
Administration and investment of funds	18
Apportionment and disposition of funds	19
Administration of school affairs in general	45
Constitutional and statutory provisions	46
Boards and officers	47
Duties of county officers and board members	48
District boards—powers and functions in general	55
Liabilities of members of district boards	62
Individual interest of member of board	62
Liabilities of district officers	63
Accounting of district officer	63
Care, maintenance, and repair of buildings	73
Contracts	77
Capacity of district to contract in general	78
Powers of district and other board officers	79
Making contracts, requisites, and validity	
Includes bids—necessity for written contracts	80
Unauthorized or illegal contracts	82
Implied contracts	83
Expenses and charges	87
Contracts especially enforced by statute	88
Power to incur expenditures	90
Constitutional and statutory power	91
Administration of finances in general	92
Appropriations	93
Payment of indebtedness in general	94
Warrants, orders, and certificates of indebtedness	95–1
In general	95–2
Issuance, requisites, and validity	95–2
Negotiability and transfer	95–3
Payments	95–4
Rights and remedies of holders	95–5
Illegal acts—Remedies of taxpayers	111

General and Sub-Headings in American Digest System

	Key Number
Counties:	
Division of school fund	157
Commission for receipt and distribution of funds	74–3
Payment by	168–1
Unauthorized contract	124–1
Recovery of money paid out	75–4
Guaranty:	
Payment of school order	30
Municipal Corporations:	
Administration of school funds	858–878
Officers	111
States:	
Limitation of Use of State Funds	119
Appropriations	131–32
Boards and Officers	94

ADDITIONAL TOPICS UNDER GENERAL HEADING "SCHOOLS AND SCHOOL DISTRICTS" SUGGESTED BY CYCLOPEDIA OF LAW AND PROCEDURE

	Vol. XXXV *Page*
Schools and School Districts—*General Heading:*	
Authority and duty to provide in general	946
Proposals and bids in general	954
Discretion of the board in making contracts	956
District expenses, charges, and statutory liability	969
Necessity for issuance of funds before issuing warrants	981
Individual liability	983
From what funds are warrants payable	986
Order of payment of warrants	986
Refunding	986

APPENDIX C

ABBREVIATIONS

A.—Atlantic Reporter
Ala.—Alabama Reports
A. L. R.—American Law Reports
Am. Dec.—American Decisions
Am. Rep.—American Reports
Ann. Cas.—Annotated Cases
Ariz.—Arizona Reports
Ark.—Arkansas Reports
A. S. R.—American State Reports

Cal.—California Reports
Cal. App.—California Appeal Reports
Colo.—Colorado Reports
Colo. App.—Colorado Appeal Reports
Conn.—Connecticut Reports
Cyc.—Cyclopedia of Law and Procedure

Del.—Delaware Reports

F.—Federal Reporter
Fla.—Florida Reports

Ga.—Georgia Reports
Ga. App.—Georgia Appeal Reports

Ia.—Iowa Reports
Ida.—Idaho Reports
Ill.—Illinois Reports
Ill. App.—Illinois Appeal Reports
Ind.—Indiana Reports

Kan.—Kansas Reports
Ky.—Kentucky Reports

La.—Louisiana Reports
La. A.—Louisiana Annual Reports
L. R. A.—Lawyers' Reports Annotated
L. R. A. n. s.—Lawyers' Reports Annotated, New Series

Mass.—Massachusetts Reports
Minn.—Minnesota Reports
Miss.—Mississippi Reports
Mo.—Missouri Reports
Mo. App.—Missouri Appeal Reports
Me.—Maine Reports
Md.—Maryland Reports
Mont.—Montana Reports

N. C.—North Carolina Reports
N. D.—North Dakota Reports
N. E.—Northeastern Reporter
Neb.—Nebraska Reports
N. H.—New Hampshire Reports
N. J. L.—New Jersey Law Reports
N. M.—New Mexico Reports
N. W.—Northwestern Reporter
N. Y.—New York Reports
N. Y. App.—New York Appeal Reports
N. Y. Misc.—New York Miscellaneous Reports
N. Y. S.—New York Supplement Reports

Okla.—Oklahoma Reports
Ore.—Oregon Reports

P.—Pacific Reporter
Pa.—Pennsylvania Reports

R. C. L.—Ruling Case Law

S. C.—South Carolina Reports
S. D.—South Dakota Reports
S. E.—Southeastern Reporter
So.—Southern Reporter
Sup. Ct.—Supreme Court Reporter
S. W.—Southwestern Reporter

Tenn.—Tennessee Reports
Tex.—Texas Reports
Tex. Civ. App.—Texas Civil Appeal Reports

U. S.—United States Supreme Court Reports

Va.—Virginia Reports
Vt.—Vermont Reports

Wash.—Washington State Reports
Wis.—Wisconsin Reports
W. Va.—West Virginia Reports
Wyo.—Wyoming Reports

SELECTED BIBLIOGRAPHY

AGGER, EUGENE. *The Budget in the American Commonwealth.* Thesis, Columbia University, Studies in History, Economics and Public Law, 1907.

ALBERTSWORTH, E. F. "Judicial Review of Administrative Action." *Harvard Law Review,* 35: 127.

ALLEN, I. M. *Teachers Contractual Status.* Contributions to Education, No. 304. Bureau of Publications, Teachers College, Columbia University, New York, 1928.

ANDERSON, E. W. *Teacher's Contract and Other Legal Phases of Teacher Status.* Contributions to Education, No. 246. Bureau of Publications, Teachers College, Columbia University, New York, 1927.

ANDERSON, WM. *American City Government.* Henry Holt and Company, New York, 1926.

ASHLEY, PERCY. *Local and Central Government: A Comparative Study of England, France, Prussia, and the United States.* E. P. Dutton and Company, New York, 1906.

BAKER, GEORGE M. "Financial Practices in Cities and Towns Below 25,000." *American School Board Journal,* No. 53. Series of Articles, December 1916 to June 1917.

BALLOU, F. W. "Efficient Finance in a City School System." *Proceedings of the National Education Association,* 1918.

BRACKETT, H. H. "Developing a Segregated School Budget." *16th Annual Report,* National Association of School Business Officials, Philadelphia, May 1926. Harrison Press, Trenton.

BROWN, W. JETHRO. *The Underlying Principles of Modern Legislation.* E. P. Dutton and Company, New York, 1915.

BRUBACKER, J. S. *Judicial Power of New York State Commissioner of Education.* Contributions to Education, No. 295. Bureau of Publications, Teachers College, Columbia University, New York, 1927.

BRUBACKER, J. S. "State Education Departments as Administrative Judicial Tribunals." *American School Board Journal,* 77: 33–36, December 1928.

BRUÈRE, HENRY. "The Budget as an Administrative Program." *Annals, the American Academy of Political and Social Science,* 62: 176–91, November 1915.

BRYCE, JAMES. *Studies in History and Jurisprudence.* Oxford University Press, American Branch, New York, 1901.

BUCK, A. E. *Municipal Finance.* .The Macmillan Company, New York, 1926.

BUCK, A. E. *Municipal Budgets and Budget Making,* National Municipal League Monograph Series, 1925.

BUCK, A. E. "The Development of the Budget Idea in the United States." *Annals, American Academy of Political and Social Science,* 113: 31–39, May 1924.

CARR, CECIL T. *Delegated Legislation.* Cambridge University Press, 1921.

CLARK, H. F. "Measuring the Budgeting Procedure of a School System." *American School Board Journal*, 68: 37–38, June 1924.

CLARK, H. F. "Suggestions for Scoring School Budgets." *American School Board Journal*, 71: 47–48, October 1925.

CLEVELAND, F. A. and BUCK, A. E. *The Budget and Responsible Government.* The Macmillan Company, New York, 1920.

CLOSE, EGBERT. "A New System of School Accounting." *American School Board Journal*, 68: 58, 123, 127, March 1924.

COOLEY, THOMAS M. *A Treatise on the Constitutional Limitations Which Rest Upon the Legislative Power of the States of the American Union.* 8th Edition, revised by Walter Carrington. (Two volumes.) Little Brown and Company, Boston, 1927.

CUBBERLEY, E. P. *State School Administration.* Houghton Mifflin and Company, Boston, 1927.

DICEY, A. V. "Development of Administrative Law in England." *Law Quarterly Review*, 31: 148–53, April 1915.

DICK, WM. "Problems in Financing a City School System." *American School Board Journal*, 70: 41–42, 1925.

DEFFENBAUGH, W. S. *Current Practice in City School Administration.* City School Leaflet No. 29, United States Bureau of Education. Government Printing Office, November 1927.

DILLON, J. F. *Commentaries on the Law of Municipal Corporations.* (5 volumes.) Little, Brown and Company, Boston, 1911.

DURANT, WILL. "Has Democracy Broken Down?" *The Forum*, Vol. 81, No. 1, January 1929.

EDWARDS, I. N. "Where and How to Find the Law Relating to Public School Administration." *Elementary School Journal*, 27: 14–24, September 1926.

EMERSON, WALLACE. "School Budgets and Budget Procedure." *American School Board Journal*, 70: 39–40, May 1925; 55: 6, June 1925; 51–2, July 1925; 52–3, August 1925.

ENGELHARDT, FRED. "Accounting Control of the Income Needs." *American School Board Journal*, September 1925.

ENGELHARDT, FRED and VON BORGERSRODE, FRED. *Accounting Procedure for School Systems.* Bureau of Publications, Teachers College, Columbia University, New York, 1927.

ENGELHARDT, N. L. and ENGELHARDT, FRED. *Public School Business Administration.* Bureau of Publications, Teachers College, Columbia University, 1927.

Fairlie, J. A. *Centralization of Administration in New York State.* Doctor's Dissertation, Columbia University, 1898.

FITZPATRICK, E. A. *Experts in City Government.* National Municipal League Series, Chap. XXIII: Beard, C. A., The Control of the Expert. D. Appleton and Company, New York, 1919.

FOWLKES, J. G. *The Accounting of Public School Expenditures in Wisconsin.* Bureau of Educational Research, Bulletin No. 4. University of Wisconsin, Madison, 1924.

FRASIER, G. W. *The Control of City School Finance.* Bruce Publishing Company, Milwaukee, 1922.

FREUND, ERNST. *Administrative Power Over Persons and Property.* University of Chicago Press, Chicago, 1928.

FREUND, ERNST. *Standards of American Legislation.* Chap. VII: The Meaning of Principle in Legislation, pp. 215–274. University of Chicago Press, Chicago, 1915.

GANDERS, HARRY S. *Personnel and Organization of Schools in Small Cities.* U. S. Bureau of Education, Bulletin, 1926, No. 6. Government Printing Office, Washington, 1926.

GOODNOW, F. J. *Comparative Administrative Law.* (Students Edition.) G. P. Putnam's Sons, New York, 1902.

GOODNOW, F. J. *The Principles of Administrative Law in the United States.* G. P. Putnam's Sons, New York, 1905.

GOODNOW, F. J. and BATES, F. G. *Municipal Government.* The Century Company, New York, 1925.

GRAY, JAMES M. *Limitations of the Taxing Power Including Limitations upon Public Indebtedness.* Bancroft-Whitney Company, San Francisco, 1906.

GRICE, J. WATSON. *National and Local Finance.* P. S. King and Son, London, 1910.

HALSEY, HENRY ROWLAND. *Borrowing Money for the Public Schools: A Study of Borrowing Practices in the Administration of Public Schools in Florida.* Contributions to Education, No. 368. Bureau of Publications, Teachers College, Columbia University, New York, 1929.

HEER, A. L. *The Present Status of Business Executives in the Public Schools of the United States in Cities of 25,000 and More Inhabitants.* Ohio State University, Columbus, 1926.

HENZLIK, F. E. *Rights and Liabilities of Public School Boards Under Capital Outlay Contracts.* Contributions to Education, No. 153. Bureau of Publications, Teachers College, Columbia University, New York, 1924.

HICKS, F. C. *Materials and Methods of Legal Research.* The Lawyer's Coöperative Publishing Company, Rochester, 1923.

HUNTER, F. M. "Efficient Expenditure of School Money." *American School Board Journal,* 76: 43–44, May 1928.

HUNTER, M. H. *Outlines of Public Finance.* Harper & Brothers, New York, 1921.

HUTCHINSON, J. H. *School Costs and Accounting.* Contributions to Education, No. 62. Bureau of Publications, Teachers College, Columbia University, New York, 1914.

Index of State Constitutions. Legislative Drafting Bureau of Columbia University. New York State Constitutional Commission, 1915.

INDIANA STATE BOARD OF ACCOUNTS. *Uniform Accounting System for School Cities and Towns:* A Handbook of Instruction. State Printer, Indianapolis, 1926.

Introduction to Reflective Thinking. (Chapter on Reflective Thinking in Law, pp. 265–300.) Columbia Associates in Philosophy. Houghton Mifflin Company, Boston, 1923.

LINN, H. H. *Safeguarding School Funds.* Contributions to Education, No. 387. Bureau of Publications, Teachers College, Columbia University, New York, 1929.

LUTZ, H. L. *Public Finance.* D. Appleton and Company. New York, 1924.

McGaughy, James R. "The Superintendent's Analysis of School Finances." *Teachers College Record*, 26: 383–93, January 1925; 660–670, April 1925.

McGaughy, James R. *Fiscal Administration of City School Systems.* Educational Finance Inquiry, Vol. V. The Macmillan Company, New York, 1924.

McGuillin, Eugene. *The Law of Municipal Corporations.* Second Edition. (7 volumes.) Callaghan and Company, Chicago, 1928.

"A Model Municipal Budget Law." Submitted by a Committee on Model Municipal Budgets, Carl H. Pforzheimer, Chairman. Supplement to *National Municipal Review*, Vol. XVII, No. 7, July 1928. National Municipal League, 261 Broadway, New York.

Moehlman, A. B. *Public School Finance.* Rand, McNally and Company, Chicago, 1927.

Moehlman, A. B. *City School Budget.* Report, Department of Superintendence of the National Education Association, Washington, 1923.

Montgomery, Robert H. *Financial Handbook.* The Ronald Press Company, New York, 1927.

Morehart, G. C. *The Legal Status of City School Boards.* Contributions to Education, No. 270. Bureau of Publications, Teachers College, Columbia University, New York, 1927.

Morris, E. L. "Status of Iowa Uniform Accounting System." *American School Board Journal*, 77: 45–46, August 1928.

Morrison, H. C. *Financing of Public Schools in the State of Illinois.* The Macmillan Company, New York, 1924.

Morrison, J. Cayce. *Legal Status of City School Superintendent.* Warwick and York, Baltimore, 1922.

Mort, Paul R. *State Support for Public Schools.* School Administration Series. Bureau of Publications, Teachers College, Columbia University, New York, 1926.

Munro, W. B. *Government of American Cities.* (New and Revised Edition.) The Macmillan Company, 1919.

Newcomer, Mabel. *Financial Statistics of Public Education in the United States*, 1910–1920. The Macmillan Company, New York, 1924.

Newcomer, Mabel. "Tendencies in State and Local Finance and Their Relation to State and Local Functions." *Political Science Quarterly*, 43: 1–31.

Oakey, F. *Principles of Government Accounting and Reporting.* Institute for Government Research. D. Appleton and Company, New York, 1921.

Orth, S. P. *The Centralization of Administration in Ohio.* Faculty of Political Science, Columbia University, New York, 1903.

Patty, W. W. "Legal Provisions for, Custody of, and Liability for Public Funds for Secondary School Support." *American School Board Journal*, 72: 47–48, March 1926; 72: 73, 130, April 1926.

Peel, A. G. *Simplified School Accounting.* Bruce Publishing Company, Milwaukee, 1925.

Peterson, Fred H. "How to Be Sure to Find the Law." *Case and Comment*, 24: 39–41, June 1927.

Pittenger, B. F. *An Introduction to Public School Finance.* Houghton Mifflin and Company, Boston, 1925.

POUND, ROSCOE. "Justice According to Law." *Columbia Law Review*, 13: 696–713; 14: 1–26.

POUND, ROSCOE. "Social and Economic Problems of the Law." *Annals, American Academy of Political and Social Science*, No. 225; 136: 1–9, March 1928.

POUND, ROSCOE. *The Present Crisis in American Law.* Harper's, 152: 152–158, January 1926.

ROWLES, W. A. *Centralizing Tendencies in the Administration of Indiana.* Columbia University Press, New York, 1903.

REEDER, WARD G. *The New Budget Law of Ohio.* Educational Research Bulletin, No. 12, Vol. V. Ohio State University, Columbus. September 1926.

SCHRAMMEL, HENRY E. *The Organization of State Departments of Education.* Bureau of Educational Research, Monograph No. 6. Ohio State University Press, Columbus, 1926.

SCIENCE OF LEGAL METHOD. *Select Essays by Various Authors.* The Macmillan Company, New York, 1921.

SEARS, JESSE B. "Some Problems in Public School Finance." *Journal of Educational Research*, 10: 257–70, November 1924.

SELIGMAN, E. R. *Studies in Public Finance.* The Macmillan Company, New York.

SLATER, C. P., and GREENE, H. A. *Administration of the School Budget.* University of Iowa Extension Bulletin, No. 122, Series 12. University of Iowa, Iowa City, April 15, 1925.

SMITH, H. P. *The Business Administration of a City School System.* Contributions to Education, No. 197. Bureau of Publications, Teachers College, Columbia University, New York, 1925.

SMITH, H. P. "Research in the Business Management of Public Schools: Progress and Problems." *American School Board Journal*, 76: 53–54, March 1928; 76: 45, April 1928.

SMITH, J. W. *Commentaries on Law of Municipal Corporations and Political Government Corporations of Every Class.* Bowen, Indianapolis, 1903.

SOPER, WAYNE. *Legal Limitations on the Rights and Powers of School Boards with Respect to Taxation.* Contributions to Education, No. 349. Bureau of Publications, Teachers College, Columbia University, 1929.

STAFFEBACH, E. H. "Financial Reports of 100 School Systems." *American School Board Journal*, 69: 32, December 1924.

STAMP, SIR JOSIAH. *Current Problems in Finance and Government.* P. S. King and Son, Ltd., London, 1924.

STOURM, RÉNÉ. *The Budget.* Translation of 7th Edition, by Thaddeus Plazinski. D. Appleton and Company, New York, 1917.

STRAYER, GEORGE D. AND ENGELHARDT, N. L. *Report of the Survey of Certain Aspects of the School System of Chattanooga and Hamilton County, Tennessee.* Bureau of Publications, Teachers College, Columbia University, New York, 1929.

STRAYER, GEORGE D. AND HAIG, R. M. *The Financing of Education in the State of New York.* Educational Finance Inquiry, Vol. I. The Macmillan Company, New York, 1923.

STRAYER, GEORGE D. "Relationship of the Executive School Officers." *American School Board Journal,* Vol. 38, August 1928.

STRAYER, GEORGE D. "Financing Public Education." Teachers College Record, 26: 145–149, 1924.

SWIFT, F. H. *Studies in Public School Finance, the East.* University of Minnesota Research Publications, Education Series, No. 2. University of Minnesota, Minneapolis, 1923.

SWIFT, F. H. *Studies in Public School Finance, the West.* University of Minnesota Research Publications, Education Series, No. 1. University of Minnesota, Minneapolis, 1922.

SWIFT, F. H. *State Policies in Public School Finance.* Bureau of Education 1922. Bulletin No. 6. Government Printing Office, Washington, 1922.

TAYLOR, R. B. *Principles of School Supply Management.* Contributions to Education, No. 228. Bureau of Publications, Teachers College, Columbia University, New York, 1926.

THEISEN, W. W. "Procedure for Uniform Accounting." *Proceedings of the 12th Annual Meeting,* National Association of Public School Business Officials, St. Louis, May 1923.

TIDWELL, CLYDE J. *State Control of Textbooks.* Contributions to Education, No. 299. Bureau of Publications, Teachers College, Columbia University, New York, 1928.

TRUSLER, H. R. *Essentials of School Law.* Bruce Publishing Company, Milwaukee, 1927.

TWENTE, J. W. *Budgetary Procedure for a Local School System.* Teachers College, Columbia University, New York, 1922.

UPSON, L. D. "Budget Making for Small Cities." *Annals, American Academy of Political and Social Science,* 62: 235–48, November 1915.

UPSON, L. D. "Half-Time Budget Methods." *Annals, American Academy of Political and Social Science,* 113: 69–74, May 1924.

UPSON, L. D. *Practice of Municipal Administration.* The Century Company, New York, 1926.

VOORHEES, H. C. *The Law of Public School System of the United States.* Little, Brown and Company, Boston, 1916.

WATSON, B. M. "Who Shall Control School Funds?" *American School Board Journal,* 65: 39–47, November 1922.

WEBB, SIDNEY. *Grants in Aid.* Longmans, Green and Company, London, 1920 Edition.

WEBER, GUSTAVONS A. *Organized Efforts for the Improvement of Administration in the United States.* D. Appleton and Company, New York, 1919.

WEHN, W. C. "Keeping School Expenditures Within the Appropriations." *American School Board Journal,* 76: 97, 149, April 1928; 75: 47, November 1927.

WHITE, LEONARD D. *Introduction to the Study of Public Administration.* The Macmillan Company, New York, 1926.

WHITTEN, R. H. *Public Administration in Massachusetts: The Relation of Central to Local Activity.* Columbia University Press, New York, 1898.

WIGMORE, J. H., AND OTHERS. *Rational Basis of Legal Institutions.* The Macmillan Company, New York, 1923.

WILLISTON, SAMUEL. *The Law of Contracts.* (5 volumes.) Baker, Voorhis and Company, New York, 1922.

WILLOUGHBY, W. F. *Principles of Public Administration:* Johns Hopkins Press, Baltimore, 1927.

WILLOUGHBY, W. F., WILLOUGHBY W. W., AND LINDSAY, S. M. *The System of Financial Administration of Great Britain.* D. Appleton and Company, New York, 1917.

WRIGHT, JOSEPH. "The City's Expenditures." Ch. XLIV, *Selected Readings in Municipal Problems.* Ginn and Company, 1925.

YOUNG, DALE S. *Control of Available Public School Income.* Contributions to Education, No. 305. Bureau of Publications, Teachers College, Columbia University, New York, 1928.

BIBLIOGRAPHIES

LEGAL

American Digest,

Century Edition, 1658–1899, Vol. XLIII.
Decennial Edition, 1897–1906, Vol. XVII.
Second Decennial Edition, 1907–1916, Vol. XX.
Key Number Series, 1917–1928, Vol. 1A–24A. Supplements, 1927 and 1928. West Publishing Company, St. Paul.

Cyclopedia of Law and Procedure, Vol. XXXV. The American Law Book Company, New York.

HICKS, F. C. *Materials and Methods of Legal Research.* The Lawyers' Coöperative Publishing Company, Rochester, 1923.

Ruling Case Law, Vol. XXIV and Supplements. Edward Thompson Company, Northport; Bancroft-Whitney Company, San Francisco; Lawyers' Coöperative Publishing Company, Rochester.

American Law Reports, Annotated, Index Volumes and Supplements. Lawyers' Coöperative Publishing Company, Rochester.

The bibliographies listed below were of great value in finding researches and opinions necessary to evaluate practices and principles discussed in this study:

PUBLIC ADMINISTRATION

GREER, SARAH. *A Bibliography of Public Administration.* National Institute of Public Administration, New York, 1926.

WILLOUGHBY, W. F. *Principles of Public Administration.* Johns Hopkins Press, Baltimore, 1927. (Excellent annotated bibliography in Appendix.)

EDUCATIONAL ADMINISTRATION

ALEXANDER, CARTER. *Bibliography on Educational Finance.* Vol. IV, Educational Finance Inquiry. The Macmillan Company, New York, 1924.

BUREAU OF EDUCATION. *Bibliography of Research Studies in Education.* U. S. Bureau of Education, Bulletin 1928, No. 22. Government Printing Office, Washington.

CLARK, HAROLD F. *A Cross-Indexed Bibliography on School Budgets.* Bulletin of the School of Education, Indiana University, Vol. II, No. 3, 1926.

ENGELHARDT, N. L. and ALEXANDER, CARTER. *School Finance and Business Management Problems.* Bureau of Publications, Teachers College, Columbia University, New York, 1928. (Chapter bibliographies.)

ENGELHARDT, N. L. and ENGELHARDT, FRED. *Public School Business Administration.* Bureau of Publications, Teachers College, Columbia University, New York, 1927. (Bibliographies at end of chapters.)

MONROE, WALTER S. and ASHER, OLLIE. *Bibliography of Bibliographies.* Bulletin No. 36. University of Illinois, Bureau of Educational Research, Urbana, 1927.

SMITH, H. P. *The Business Administration of a City School System.* Contributions to Education, No. 197. Bureau of Publications, Teachers College, Columbia University, New York, 1925.

STRAYER, GEORGE D., ENGELHARDT, N. L., et al. *Problems in Educational Administration.* Bureau of Publications, Teachers College, Columbia University, New York, 1925. (Bibliographies to problems in Sections III, IV, and V.)

Ten Years of Educational Research, 1918–1927. Bulletin No. 42. University of Illinois, Bureau of Educational Research, Urbana, 1928.

SOURCES OF LEGAL MATERIALS

American Decisions
Bancroft-Whitney Company, San Francisco

American Reports
Bancroft-Whitney Company, San Francisco

American State Reports
Bancroft-Whitney Company, San Francisco

Federal Reports

National Reporter System, West Publishing Company, St. Paul:
- Atlantic Reporter
- Northeastern Reporter
- Northwestern Reporter
- Pacific Reporter
- Southeastern Reporter
- Southern Reporter
- Southwestern Reporter

State Reporter Systems

State Codes of the Various States

Statutes and Session Laws of the Various states.